THE
FORBIDDEN
TREE:

History or Folklore?

Is the Bible Really the Infallible Word of God?

Jabulani Midzi

authorHOUSE®

AuthorHouse™ UK
1663 Liberty Drive
Bloomington, IN 47403 USA
www.authorhouse.co.uk
Phone: 0800.197.4150

Published by AuthorHouse 08/05/2016

ISBN: 978-1-5246-6191-5 (sc)
ISBN: 978-1-5246-6190-8 (e)

Print information available on the last page.

DEDICATION

I dedicate this book to all generations of mankind: past, present, and future. It is my fervent hope that it will resonate with their deepest aspirations and yearnings for liveable truth that resides deep in their subconscious minds and is engraved on the tablets of their hearts.

CONTENTS

INTRODUCTION

As we are presently living in the so-called information age and preparing ourselves for an informed future, we would like to address the misinformation of past generations. We will consolidate that which is true and courageously reject misconceptions presented in whatever guise. In this book, we would like to self-introspect and to fairly and openly question and verify the claims about the Christian Bible being the holy word of God.

May I invite you to open yourself up to the possibility of learning something new: not necessarily something absolutely new but eternal truths tucked away in the dark corners of your own consciousness and 'gathering dust', as it were. All universal truths are an irrevocable part of our DNA. You will hear some things that you already know. You may also be awakened to some things that were brought to you before; however, you either silenced those soft voices or blamed yourself for being too inquisitive. I am referring to things that were brought to you by your intuition and that do not add up logically.

A lot has been said. A lot has been written. And I suppose a lot shall continue to occupy our minds and dominate our interactions as humans regarding the claim that the Christian Bible is the 'word of God'.

I have made a number of observations about the various claims regarding the major themes of the Christian Bible. However, it is very important that I mention to the reader that these observations are not meant to be judgements. If an observation does not resonate with your core being, it should not be regarded as a painful collision, but rather just a difference in opinion. You are free to choose your response to it. If it resonates with your deepest truths, you are equally free to choose how to respond. Just remember this golden rule: *An observation is not a judgement.*

Therefore, feel free to disagree with anything found herein. At the same time, I urge you to have the courage to agree with that which is in harmony with your intuition and the great campus of common sense which binds us all together.

The major themes we would like to examine are as follows:

1. the theory of the fall of man
2. the story of creation
3. the theory of heaven and hell
4. mankind's need for salvation
5. folklore in the Bible
6. belief versus knowledge
7. punishment and forgiveness

One of the greatest endowments humans have is the freedom to choose how they want to experience any aspect of life. They choose by using their common sense and, to a large extent, their willpower. This is the universal principle that is available to all. A common denominator. This common sense is influenced by the logic they derive from natural laws and principles in the observable universe. As a result, almost all human inventions are based on logic.

When natural laws are in action, they produce natural consequences. For example, under gravitational conditions, if you place a 1-kilogram concrete brick on top of a ripe tomato, the tomato will be squashed. However, if the same tomato were to be placed on top of that same brick, nothing would happen. Both would keep their original state. Simple logic.

If a human being places a hot coal in his mouth, the tongue and other parts of the mouth would be burnt, and it is usually painful. The burns and pain are the natural consequences. Natural consequences are predetermined and are not subject to choice. Humans can choose to utilise these consequences for 'good' or for 'evil', to reward or to punish. So man can choose to act but cannot choose the natural consequence of the action.

However, if people adjudge the actions of an individual to be either favourable or unfavourable, they might decide to reward or punish the actor if they can. Reward is meant to encourage, and punishment is meant to discourage future action. Both are called reinforcement and are positive and negative, respectively. What is critical to note is that reinforcement has no natural link to the action but is subject to the interests and decisions of another being. People can decide to reward or to punish.

If this cycle of response – reward/punishment – is repeated long enough, it creates a form of conditioning. In a way, the freedom to choose becomes corrupted by the power of conditioning. The surest way to kill a human being is to disarm him or her of common sense and replace it with conditioning, especially if you can convince the said person that it is ungodly to use common sense.

Today, when an ordinary person holds and reads the Christian Bible, the dominant assumption is that it is God's holy book and the word of God, the creator. This has been brought about by incessant teaching and indoctrination by the church. The cornerstone of this indoctrination is discouragement from using common sense to evaluate claims but using belief as a basis for decision-making. People are told that the Bible was written by God through inspiration to the authors. This has led to everything written in the Bible being referred to as the infallible word of God, including poems and folklore.

My observation is that not everything in the Bible was written by God and is absolute truth. Rather, some writings are legendary stories based on the authors' misconceptions about God and the universe at that time, some of which have since become obsolete. I also observe that the main themes of the Bible would seem to actually distort and misrepresent the character of God. God is portrayed as vindictive, insecure, untruthful, weak, unforgiving, and even hypocritical.

We would like to establish the truth value of these assertions. Let us start with folklore in the Bible that is labelled as historical events.

Chapter 1

FOLKLORE IN THE BIBLE

It is generally accepted by both scholars and the church that biblical writings fall into six basic categories:

- the law
- history
- poetry
- prophecy
- the gospels
- epistles

Let us first acknowledge the importance of dividing the Bible into these categories in the first place. Categorizing writings is of huge importance because it assigns them the level of authority with which they should be regarded. For example, poetry and the law are weighted differently in the event of a controversial subject. In like manner, Solomon's poem will not carry the same weight as a clear 'thus says the Lord' statement in the Torah if they appear to be at variance. Likewise, Paul's opinion on marriage in one of his epistles will not carry the day if pitted against

'God's law' that says, 'Be fruitful and multiply'. Therefore the category in which a writing is placed determines the level of authority it has, which further determines whether it can be questioned and debated or has a take-it-or-leave-it status.

I would like to introduce to the reader the existence of another category of Bible writings: folklore. This is not to be confused with parables. I call it the 'hidden category' because no attempt was ever made to refer to it openly, although the compilers knew it was there. They deliberately dissolved folklore into other categories. The reason for that is quite suspicious, which we will explore in a moment. For now, let us quickly look at comparisons between folklore and parables. Folklore encompasses folk tales, fables, animal tales, legends, myths, fairy tales, and the like. It differs from a parable in that folklore may employ anything from humans, animals, plants, inanimate objects, or forces of nature as characters, whereas parables have only humans as main characters. A parable is basically a type of analogy, whereas folklore may be regarded as a symbolic representation of folk belief and collective experiences and reaffirms commonly held values of the society to whose tradition it belongs.

Folklore and parables have one thing in common, though: They are both imaginary creations of the mind using existing knowledge as reference. They are not historical events. They never actually happened. They are primarily meant to reinforce a lesson or a principle.

Apart from carrying a lesson or reinforcing a principle, folklore has a unique extra dimension. It seeks to explore the origins of the current reality and then creatively speculate on what might have caused things to be the way they are, especially things that concern our ecosystem, such as the behavioural patterns and relationships amongst animal species, humans, and their environment. It may seek to explain why certain animals feed on others, why they behave in certain ways, and so on.

Different cultures have different versions of how things began and evolved to what they are now. This is captured in the different, and sometimes similar, folk tales, legends, and fables in our respective cultures. There is one critical aspect that all cultures do not forget to teach their children, which is that these tales are not historical events. At best, they are just creative speculation. They make sure their children capture that. Although in most cases children take the tales as actual history, society ensures that they eventually know the truth – the eternal truth – that these stories are simply imaginary creative tales. People pass them on to the next generation as such.

Folk tales were a form of admission by our forebears that they did not know how life started. Even now, it seems God has not revealed it to anyone. Humans back then could speculate, and they can only speculate even now. The Big Bang theory, the Darwinian theory of evolution, the story of creation in the Jewish scriptures, and many other cultural legends tussle with each other to occupy this void. None of them is the absolute truth, nor is it supposed to be. They are all results of the creativity of the human mind. It is all speculation. Humanity does not know how all things were created. Only God knows. So far, it seems he has not yet revealed it to humans. Frankly, there is no need to.

As noted earlier, classification of some biblical writings as folklore seems to have been deliberately omitted. I strongly suspect that the scholars and church fathers who compiled the Bible dissolved this category knowingly for religious expedience. As a result, some folk tales, legends, and fables were taught, and are still being taught, as actual historical events. But actual history happened in the realm of space and time and was governed by natural laws and principles. History happens in total harmony with these natural laws and principles. There is no contradiction, except, of course, in the rare case of a miracle.

What the compilers seem to have ignored is that once folklore is presented as material fact, then it provokes the need to establish its truth value. To do that, the logic of all its inferences and insinuations is scrutinised to ascertain its relation to absolute truth.

Another possibility is that the compilers of the Bible genuinely thought that biblical folklore was literal history; however, there cannot be any excuse for such recklessness, considering the importance of the job that was before them.

In my view, there are folk tales, myths, legends, and fables in the Bible, but all of them seem to have been deliberately hidden inside other categories. As a result, when those stories considered as historical events are scrutinised and measured against the yardstick of natural principles and absolute truth, they simply collapse like a house of cards. We will pick a few examples for scrutiny. These are the story of Job, the fall of man, the story of creation, and the Tower of Babel.

The book of Job is a prime example of a legend. For all the excitement that the story of Job generates, it is hard for most people to understand that it is folklore. It is not a historical narrative. The famed meeting between God and Satan to discuss Job and the so-called agreement for testing him is not literal history. The story of Job did not happen. It is not history. It was a legend that was meant to teach people not to conclude that when misfortune befalls a person, that person must have sinned. It localizes the romantic story in a definite spot: the land of Uz.

The story of Job is classified as poetry in the Bible, but it is a legendary poem. Like all legends, it has the characteristics of a historical event. It is repeatedly taught in churches as a historical event, and there is total silence about the fact that it is a legend. Humankind is made to believe that the story of Job is a historical event, so people are left thinking that there was an actual meeting between God and his sons, including Lucifer, and that a plot to tempt Job was hatched there. Research shows that the author of the book is unknown and the ancestry of the main character, Job, is also unknown. The books is regarded as poetry because clearly it cannot fit anywhere in the history of Israel. It is not history: It is a creative composition. However, because to openly disclose that it is a legend would cause a lot of ramifications, it is cunningly classified as poetry. The integrity of the compilers is compromised in the process.

The book of Genesis suffered the same fate as Job. It is classified as part of the Law—the Torah or the Pentateuch. However, some chapters, such as the story of creation, the fall of man, and the Tower of Babel, are folklore whose authors are largely unknown. In fact, chapters 1 to 11 are a mixture of fables, legends, myths, and even tall tales, but chapter 12 onwards would seem to qualify more as history.

One major characteristic of folklore is its lack of a conclusive origin or authorship. It is hard to tell who started the story and when. Usually, the last-known most influential person in the relevant society gets credited as the originator. In the Bible's case, there is a spirited attempt to speculate that Genesis was written by Moses. However, doubts about Moses's authorship of the Pentateuch abound, as scholars are not in agreement. The last five verses of Deuteronomy add to the confusion. The most prominent question is how Moses could write about his own burial. We will take a closer look at these legends of Genesis later.

For now, let us look at a classical example of an African cultural fable: the story of the owl as king of the birds.

CHAPTER 2

THE OWL: KING OF THE BIRDS

Legend has it that once upon a time, the great horned owl was king of all birds. It goes like this …

In the beginning of time, the great horned owl was the king of the birds. He was a ruthless king. He decreed that every morning, each bird must bring him food – anything ranging from locusts and worms to rats and the like. He claimed that he was special and had been chosen by God to rule them. To secure his kingdom, he claimed that his feather tufts were actually two horns and enforced compliance to his orders by threating to gore and kill any disobedient bird.

The birds lived in fear and religiously carried out the task of feeding King Owl. It went on for quite a long time until all the birds from one generation to the next accepted this as gospel truth that King Owl had horns and would kill any bird who did not comply with his orders or dared to question his claim to the throne. King Owl was revered and feared. No bird would even consider touching his 'holy' body or coming close to the throne.

In the meantime, King Owl kept his big lie as a closely guarded secret. As time passed by, however, complacence crept in, and King Owl began to invite some 'small, harmless' birds to scratch his back when it itched and to search for lice and other parasites underneath his feathers. He enjoyed this, and he usually fell asleep during these massages. This went on for quite some time without incident. He encouraged the birds to search diligently and thoroughly under the feathers to make sure he was free from parasites.

Then one day, it was the fork-tailed drongo Nhengure's turn to massage the king while searching for parasites. The bird was meticulous, paying attention to detail as he went from feather to feather. He was not suspicious at all but genuinely wanted to follow the king's order to be diligent.

Nhengure was a friend to cattle and he often fed on parasites such as ticks and big flies that live on cattle blood. He had discovered that, at the base of cattle horns, there are some scales that peel off as the horns grow, which he removed regularly.

As Nhengure went about his job, King Owl enjoyed it so much that, as usual, he fell asleep. When Nhengure remembered the scales that peel off at the roots of cattle horns, he decided to check to see if the owl had a similar problem. He was nervous about getting too close to the king's revered horns but felt duty-bound to do a thorough job.

To get to the root of the horn, he had to push aside all the feathers surrounding the horn without hurting the king. So the meticulous Nhengure started. He moved one feather, another feather, another feather, more feathers, and then the feathers started to become bigger, longer, and thicker. He went on and on, but still no sign of a horn or its root. He kept going, but the feathers began to decrease in size. Focused on his goal, he kept going until he realized that he had actually passed the first 'horn' and that the second one was fast approaching. He did not think much of it. Neither did he take time to digest what had just entered his consciousness.

He proceeded with the same due diligence to the second 'horn', but the same thing happened. He took a deep breath in disbelief. Still not sure what to make of all this, he double-checked both 'horns' and was shocked by the discovery. He carried on with his work as if nothing unusual had happened. King Owl was snoring by now. Nhengure finished his duty and left without saying a thing. He needed time to digest what he had discovered and, most importantly, to chart the way forward. For sure he had seen enough to make up his mind.

The following morning at the assembly, King Owl issued the routine instruction for all birds to bring him fresh food and for someone else to massage him after feeding. But, to the surprise of all the birds and King Owl himself, Nhengure stood up and openly defied King Owl's order. Lifting his wing and pointing at his own chest, he said, 'I am not going to bring you food. I won't do it today and I never will again!' Before the owl could respond, the birds tried to restrain Nhengure and asked him to withdraw his words, but he refused. The owl rose up in anger and, in a thunderous voice, described how he was going to gore Nhengure to death mercilessly. At that instant, Nhengure, in a fit of rage, flew towards the owl shouting, 'I know you do not have horns. These are just feathers!' So saying, he sunk his beak into the root of one of King Owl's tufts. Realizing that the cat had been let out of the bag, the owl fled the scene with Nhengure in hot pursuit.

King Owl went and hid in a cave. Nhengure then returned to the gathered birds and explained to them how they had been duped by owl for all that time. He vowed to strike the owl whenever and wherever he met him.

From that day on, the owl did not hunt during daylight. It became a bird of the night. That is why if it appears during daylight, the fork-tailed drongo will strike it and chase it back to the caves.

What a story. A fable and not a historical event. If one claimed that this fable were a historical event, and if it were to be scrutinised and measured against the yardstick of natural principles and absolute truth, it would simply crumble. There would be many unanswerable questions. However, as a fable, it is truly a masterpiece.

Let us now explore folklore in the Bible. There is no better place to start than the fall of man.

CHAPTER 3

THE FALL OF MAN: WHO LIED, GOD OR SATAN?

We would like to explore the fall of man narrative found in Genesis 3 to determine whether it is legendary or historical. We will also examine the implications of taking it as a fable as opposed to an historical event.

One of the most fascinating stories found in the Bible is about how mankind purportedly 'fell from grace'. According to the narrative, mankind disobeyed God's command and was subsequently condemned to death. It then goes further to claim that God cursed the earth, which resulted in animals starting to kill each other for food plus a long list of other unsavoury 'consequences'.

To begin with, we will start with the question of who lied and who told the truth between God and Satan. We need to free ourselves from any prejudice and objectively look at the facts as they are presented in the narrative with our common sense fully engaged. Like in the court of law, competent judges restrict themselves to the facts as presented by both the prosecution and the defence council. The greatest temptation is the lure of getting influenced by their own prejudices. However, the great endowment of self-awareness should come to the judge's rescue. For instance, if a female judge is presiding over a rape case, it is critically important that she constantly monitor her own emotional attachment to the case by virtue of being a woman. Failure to do that may lead her into passing a partial and emotionally charged sentence.

I urge you to listen to your inner self, to your own voice, to your intuition as you read these passages. Your common sense is probably the most important tool that the creator endowed you with as a human being. That sets us apart from the rest of the animal kingdom.

Let us examine 'the fall of man'. There is no better place to start than Genesis 2: 16–17 and Genesis 3: 4–7. NIV.

> 2 16 And the LORD God commanded the man, 'You are free to eat from any tree in the garden; 17 but you must not eat from the tree of the knowledge of good and evil, for when you eat from it you will certainly die.'

> 3 4 'You will not certainly die,' the serpent said to the woman. 5 'For God knows that when you eat from it your eyes will be opened, and you will be like God, knowing good and evil.'

God's message to man: When you eat from the tree, you will certainly die.

Serpent's message to man: When you eat from the tree, you will not certainly die. God knows that your eyes will be opened, and you will be like God, knowing good and evil.

> ³ ⁶ When the woman saw that the fruit of the tree was good for food and pleasing to the eye, and also desirable for gaining wisdom, *she took some and ate it. She also gave some to her husband, who was with her, and he ate it.* ⁷ *Then the eyes of both of_them were opened, and they realized they were naked;* so they sewed fig leaves together and made coverings for themselves (emphasis added).

Let us expose this passage to the scrutiny of an historical event and examine what actually happened after they ate the fruit. It can be observed that

1. They did not die.
2. Their eyes were opened.
3. They 'realised' they were naked. That is. they now knew evil and good.
4. Hence they became like God – knowing good and evil.

Exactly what the serpent had said. All four points to Satan and zero to God so far.

Of interest to note here is that the 'serpent' never said anything again after the man had 'sinned'. Only God had something to say. Why?

Let us examine what God said after man ate the fruit:

> ³ ²² And the LORD God said, '*The man has now become like one of us, knowing good and evil.* He

must not be allowed to reach out his hand and *take also from the tree of life and eat, and live forever*' (emphasis added).

Crucially, God does not say, 'Now the man has died; let us make a plan to save him.' Instead he says, 'The man has now become like one of us, knowing good and evil.' He is confirming what the serpent, the so-called 'devil', had said God knew would happen. It also confirms that, all along, man was not like God because he did not know good and evil. After all, this particular tree was designed to give the ability to have knowledge of good and evil and, with that, the freedom of choice. In other words, man was incomplete when he was created. He was still a work in progress. He was like a baby and had no idea whatsoever of good and evil. He also did not live forever. He would only live forever after eating from the tree of life. Surely, from the given information, man was not like God when he was created.

It is quite evident that one could only acquire the ability to know good and evil by eating the fruit from the tree of the knowledge of good and evil. At the time of 'committing the crime', Adam and his wife had not yet eaten from that tree. Therefore they certainly did not have the capacity to know good and evil. The question is, how then can a sane God give a commandment to someone who has no capacity to know good and evil? God knew very well that the capacity to know good and evil would only be installed in man through eating the fruit of knowledge.

Let me use a computer analogy here. The central processing unit (CPU) of a computer works a bit like the human brain. It only utilizes software that is already installed. If, for example, antivirus software is not installed, then the computer has no capacity to detect and fight viruses. If Microsoft Office is not installed, you should not expect your computer to produce an Excel spread sheet.

To veer from computers, if a war pilot's lenses are not fitted with night vision capability, surely the commander cannot expect him to see in the dark. If your gun is not fitted with a silencer, it will make noise and you will be detected.

This human being was not wired to know good and evil. The software for such was not yet installed. Concepts such as good, evil, death, fear, threat, punishment, wisdom, and foolishness meant nothing to man at that stage. He was a baby, and God knew this when he gave the command. Worse still, he goes on to threaten the ignorant guy with death: something the man has no concept of. Death meant nothing to Adam at that stage, nor did something called 'disobedience'. As he was a newborn baby, fear did not exist. As we all know, a baby can crawl straight off a cliff or into a burning fire. Surely you cannot instruct babies not to touch fire by simply telling them that they will burn. Burning means nothing to the baby until the 'software' about burning is installed later.

Another example: If you buy a brand-new smartphone, it does not come with all apps. If you want to use WhatsApp, you must first install it onto your phone. Only then can you start messaging. In other words, you need to be sure that the phone is capable of processing the command before you issue it. How could God then do such a dull thing? Issuing a command to a brain he knew very well had no capacity to process it would have been strange, to be sure.

Please note: The 'software' for the ability to know good and evil and the ability to live forever were not installed when man was created. They were supposed to be 'downloaded' from the two trees. He was supposed to install these by eating fruit from the two respective trees. The two trees were in the middle of the garden. Initially only one tree was prohibited: the tree of knowledge of good and evil. There was no instruction not to eat from the tree of life. It was only *after* man ate from the tree of knowledge that God blocked access to the tree of life. It would seem that God was prepared to let man live forever as long as he did not know good and evil. If man had eaten the fruit from the tree of life first, there was no problem, as long as he did not eat from the tree of knowledge. To eat from both could have been God's greatest nightmare.

Even more crucially, the follow-up statement in the narrative (3: 22) brutally exposes God. He clearly demonstrates that he did not want man to be like him – that is, to know good and evil and also live forever. He had to do something as a matter of urgency to save himself, not to save man. He must prevent man from accessing the tree of life. All along, God was not concerned about man eating the fruit of the tree of life as long as he knew no evil and good: as long as he was just a stooge, a robot. But now everything drastically changes after man's eyes are opened. Does it seem God is pressing the panic button here? I think so. He is clearly frantic. Certainly this is *not* one of the attributes of God. This can only be folklore.

God is clearly portrayed here as insecure, worried, and restless. And God, for the first time, acknowledges that man has only now become like one of them (God) – but only in one respect: to know good and evil. Luckily for God, man is still mortal because he has not yet eaten from the tree of life. So to save himself, God must quickly prevent man from eating the fruit of the tree of life; otherwise, he truly becomes another God – knowing good and evil *and* living forever.

Surely, if the devil were on a mission to fix God, he could have made sure that man ate both fruits in quick succession. By the time God came in the cool of the evening, the game would have been long over. Who would miss such a glorious opportunity?

Of course, it was not to be. That is the stuff folk tales and legends are made of. It is like watching a horror film in which you wish you could advise an actor that he is about to be ambushed. Folklore will always have glaring gaps. A fable does not pay attention to material detail: It is mainly concerned with manufacturing the desired outcome.

If the God depicted above is supposed to be the Supreme Being, then I am lost. Surely I find it extremely difficult to reconcile. Thus far, it is clear that man was created as a mortal being. He would only attain immortality after eating fruit from the tree of life. And God is said to have denied him that chance. Therefore, it seems incorrect to say or imply that man became mortal because of 'sin' (eating the fruit). Rather man is mortal because he was created mortal and did not eat the fruit of the tree of life. The capability to live forever was never installed in his system. The physical man was never designed to live forever. He had a lifespan, and that had nothing to do with sin. Therefore, physical death is actually desirable. Only premature death is undesirable. Even as God is said to have made a covenant with Abram, one of His promises was that Abram would go to his ancestors in peace and be buried at a ripe old age.

I have observed that anything in the physical realm that reproduces itself has a lifespan. It is born, matures, reproduces, and then dies to leave space for its offspring to thrive in. Imagine if every person that ever lived was still alive. Every fly, every lion, every dog, every bird, all creatures. Living forever and reproducing continually. How irresponsible would it have been for God to create the world so? Surely there must be something wrong with this version of creation if it were to be taken literally. However, as a fable, it is a masterpiece.

There are numerous such stories from different other non Judeo-Christian cultures, but they do not teach their children that these are literal historical events. They never tell the world to take their legends as bona fide words of God. They do not promise life to those who believe and death to those who dare to question or simply refuse to believe them. They do not claim to have a monopoly on the knowledge of God. They do not live in order to go to heaven. They do not claim to be the chosen nation, though they acknowledge that they are an irreplaceable part of a great whole.

As seen here by God's own admission, man could go on and live forever if God had left him to reach out to the tree of life. By implication, if man had eaten the fruit of life before or immediately after eating the fruit of knowing evil and good, there was nothing God could do about it. There would be two more Gods. Period. Man would have lived forever while also knowing good and evil.

How then does the notion that man was made in the likeness of God fare in these unfolding events? Judging by what we have seen so far, it seems as if it is not a statement *by* God that man was made in the likeness of God. It looks increasingly like a statement made by man through the fertility of his imagination. God is probably not like man in form and shape. What is clear, though, is that man was endowed with authority on earth. However, to speculate that man was made in the image and likeness of God is far-fetched, especially when it is presented as history. If it is a fable, yes. We can claim to be like God.

Let us now look deeply at immortality itself and how it is portrayed in this narrative.

CHAPTER 4

IS IMMORTALITY REVERSIBLE?

It would seem from the biblical God's own words and frantic actions that, once attained, immortality is irreversible. It is evident that after mankind ate the fruit, God's biggest concern became that of preventing man from living forever while also knowing good and evil. Therefore, God had to quickly organise cherubim with flaming swords to guard the way to the tree of life, and he had to eject man from the garden.

One wonders where all this desperation stems from if immortality is reversible. I once thought man could eat from the tree of life and God could still kill him if he wanted to. I was wrong. Immortality cannot be revoked in the same way academic qualifications or other accolades, such as honorary degrees and knighthood are revoked. Immortality is permanent. No immortal being can become mortal again. Only mortal beings can be elevated to immortality. God knew that if man could eat the fruit from the tree of life, he would live forever, regardless of whether God liked it or not. It would be beyond God's control, as it were, simply because the power to live forever was vested in the tree of life and God would not interfere with that. He delegated that authority to the tree, and he respected that 'separation of power', so to speak. Therefore, it appears that even God cannot reverse immortality once attained.

On the other hand, if immortality *could* be reversed, then that would mean immortality is also mortal. Immortality would essentially cease to exist. As long as there is the potential to die or for life to be reversed, then immortality, as a reality, becomes null and void. That, by extension, would mean that even God himself would have the potential to die. He becomes mortal. Luckily, here in this account, God seems to endorse the notion that immortality is irreversible.

This is also true of the knowledge of good and evil. Once the man ate the fruit, their eyes were opened, and God never attempted to 'close' them again. Instead he accepted the new reality and went along with it, even though he did not like it. He had to make clothes for them in response to their newly acquired state of knowing good and evil. Man had graduated from being like an ordinary animal to being like God. The tree had done its job, and man, for the first time, became aware of something called nakedness. I would speculate that if that fruit were to be given to any other animal, it would achieve the same result and that animal would scurry for cover to hide its nakedness. Just imagine all the dogs, cattle, and other wild animals becoming aware of their nakedness and looking around for ways to cover themselves. Surely there would be pandemonium.

That brings up the interesting question regarding the mortality of Satan and Jesus as God. Can God really be killed? How could God be killed on the cross? Unless of course he pretended to die. If Jesus of Nazareth is indeed God, as many people passionately claim, then surely he never died because God *cannot* die. God is immortal and immortality is irreversible. There is no such thing as oscillating between immortality and mortality. Today one is immortal, tomorrow mortal, and the next day immortal again? Never. Except in fiction and in folklore. Then, yes.

Therefore to claim that God became flesh and put on mortality must rank as one of the biggest hoaxes of our time. No immortal being can be made mortal, except by pretence. But, wait a minute, can God pretend? The answer is an emphatic no. Not the Supreme Being, of course; not the holy one. Never. But in folklore and fiction? Yes.

Therefore, the Bible seems to accuse God of pretence. This is the irony of all ironies. Just picture this: It is claimed that there was war in heaven, wherever that 'place' may be. God was fighting against the rebel angels led by Lucifer. It was a war of ideas or words, but certainly not of physical weapons, we are told. The question is, was God fighting for real or pretending to fight? Let us say he was pretending to fight with his creature Lucifer. He eventually prevails, but not quite. He has to find a new home for the vanquished rebel and his army. Very responsible and considerate of him –magnanimous, even. He throws him 'down' onto earth, the dwelling place of one of his innocent creatures, mankind. What is God thinking? He himself cannot put up with the rebels, but he expects man to live together with them. Has God become insane?

The man on earth knows no evil. Neither does he know good. Remember man has not yet eaten from the tree of knowledge. He is just like any other animal. God knows fully well that man is still a baby and is no match for the 'devil'. Nonetheless, he throws Satan and his followers to contaminate the then pure earth. How irresponsible of him?

Satan did not come to earth voluntarily. He was thrown there by God himself. By extension, God deliberately brought sin to an innocent earth. This is contrary to common wisdom. Sin is like cancer. If cancer is found in one of your legs, for example, the most logical thing to do is to cut off the leg before the cancer spreads. People do not transfer the cancer cells to an uninfected part of the body in order to test the body.

The earth and the so-called heaven are parts of the same universe. So that would mean that Lucifer was simply transferred from one part to another part of the same universe. Why then claim that Satan was defeated when in actual fact it was just a transfer of the battleground. In fact, it was the expansion of the battleground because there is still no peace in heaven. Even up to this day, we are told there is sadness. Angels are being sent on reconnaissance missions and bringing back reports – sorrowful reports of man's suffering. The war still rages on. Heaven is the command centre, and earth is now the war zone. God is the commander-in-chief of his army. Or is it Michael the archangel? One thing for certain is that the war is far from over – if ever there was a war.

We are also told that God does not deal decisively with Satan by killing him in heaven because he wants to demonstrate to all creation that he is just and fair. Even humanity is said to eventually testify with their mouths that God's judgements are true and just. From this it seems that God is now concerned about being judged by humans to such an extent that he allows 'evil' to reign in order for him to be vindicated and prove his innocence. What an insecure God. Surely this can only be folklore, but let us continue to take it as literal history for a while longer.

Can Satan really be killed? Again, the answer is no. He is a spiritual, immortal being. Let us be generous and say he was mortal at the time he talked to Eve. Surely, with all his knowledge and cunningness as described in the narrative, we can see that he could eat from the tree of life, which was so close to him as they conversed. I speculate that he would have eaten from it. That is, if he were mortal. We are told he was an angel, and angels are immortal beings. When then did he become mortal if immortality cannot be reversed? How does God hope to kill Lucifer the devil with fire? How do you kill death (the so-called last enemy to be killed) with fire? The only way to kill death is to resurrect everybody and keep them alive forever. If you kill the sinners, then, as long as they are dead, death exists. How can you destroy sin with fire? All these entities are spiritual, but fire is a physical entity. Seeing this contradiction, we are now told that the devil and his followers will be tormented in hell for eternity. Of what benefit is this eternal torment to God? Folk tales are made of stuff like this.

If God acknowledged that he could not kill a person after he had eaten from the tree of life, then how can someone teach that immortal beings can be killed? God shows the way when the best solution for him was to prevent man from accessing the tree of life. Prevention was better than a cure. Now God can kill mankind at will because they are mortal. This presents God as very insecure.

As if to acknowledge that immortal beings cannot be killed, the writers invented another concept: a hell burning for eternity. The 'devil' and his followers are to burn in hellfire for eternity. One continues to wonder, of what benefit to God would be their pain?

The eternal question still is this: Is God fighting a real war or he is just pretending to fight? If he is pretending, then the Bible further insinuates that God pretended to be a baby in a human womb, pretended to be a man, pretended to be weak enough to be captured by humans, pretended to die so that he could then pretend to have risen from the dead, pretended to have defeated physical death and ultimately pretended to have purchased reconciliation with mankind although there was no separation in the first place. Man never sinned against God because he had no capacity to choose.

The very fact that he is purported to have stayed in the human womb and lived among humanity testifies that he was never separated from man at all. This idea that God separated with man after man 'sinned' is probably another bad hoax. God could only be pretending. But then, does God ever pretend? Either way, something does not add up about his character and attributes. This can only be folklore.

I assume that it is common knowledge across all monotheistic cultures that God, the Supreme Being, is too powerful to engage in a real fight with anything, let alone against his own creatures. It is a mismatch. He does not win or lose. Yes, you read that right: God is neither a winner nor a loser because God has no competitor. He is the all in all, lacking nothing. He is not needy. He is all-powerful. Unless, of course, if he is pretending to be weak.

The so-called war between God and Satan is clearly non-existent. It is absolutely impossible. Therefore it can only be a figment of humanity's fertile imagination. It is based on misconceptions about God at best and blatant deception at worst. There is no war between God and Satan, whether in the past, present, or future. It is impossible. God fighting a real war against his creature? Or simulating war? Impossible. Humanity must just be kidding. It is folklore.

All this is fuelled by misconceptions regarding the relationship between the so-called good and the so-called evil. They are thought to be at war, hence the need to personify them as God and Satan.

Let us unpack this further.

CHAPTER 5

IS THERE A WAR BETWEEN GOOD AND EVIL?

Another misconception, which is probably the root of humanity's problems, is that there is war between good and evil. In a very shallow context, it may appear to be so, but not in the grand scheme of things. Good and evil are never at war, never have been, and never shall be. They are two sides of the same coin, and no coin has only one side. They find meaning in each other. Therefore, a place where only good dwells can only be a myth at best.

That is why God inspired Albert Einstein to reveal the general theory of relativity. In the absence of evil, good is not. And in the absence of good, evil is not. Good defines evil, and evil defines good. They lean on each other to get balance. They complement each other and are never at war. That they are at war is a human illusion. Their harmony is the essence of divinity.

You cannot experience good as good without the awareness of evil. Likewise, you cannot experience evil as evil without the awareness of good. It is like light and darkness. To experience light as light, one must be aware of the experience of darkness, and vice versa. Darkness is simply the absence of light. You cannot remove light and also remove darkness at the same time in the same space. Impossible. Without hot, there is no cold; without low, there is no high; without short, there is no tall; without far, there is no near; without fat, there is no thin. The list is endless. Ultimately, the whole human experience is relative. It is a relationship between so-called opposite conditions, aptly summed up as good and evil, God and Satan, or heaven and hell.

The same applies to the law and sin. They exist because of each other. The law defines sin. Without the law, there is no sin. Without the desire to define sin, there is no need for the law. There is no order. The moment you create order, you automatically define disorder. The moment you enact a law, you create the potential for sin. In fact, by enacting a law, you define the parameters for sin. They are not at war but they define each other. They exist together separately, but they act together in a permanent pattern in an unbreakable cycle. They are two pieces of one garment joined together seamlessly. They are like a husband and wife, seemingly opposite but one in marriage. It is what Neale Donald Walsch calls 'a divine dichotomy'.

Let me put it this way: That which humans call 'good' is actually half-God, and that which people call 'evil' is in fact the other half-God. They exist together side by side from eternity past to eternity future. They are jointly exhaustive and mutually exclusive. Combine them and you have God. Try to separate them, and you have good and evil, heaven and hell. It is a human creation. A delusion.

Currently, humans describe Satan as a fallen angel, a creature, but they also give him the characteristics of God the creator. One of the attributes of God often attributed to Satan is omnipresence. It would seem that he is everywhere in the universe where God is. He is depicted as omniscient because he seems to know whatever God knows and is always ready with a convenient counterfeit. The truth of the matter is that wherever God is, there is good and evil. Good plus evil equals God (good + evil = God). Likewise, heaven + hell = paradise.

It is like the state of equilibrium. Remember Newton's third law of motion: for every action, there is an equal and opposite reaction. I submit that Newton was inspired by the Supreme Being to reveal this. Therefore, sin did not start in the heart of Lucifer, as some claim. No. Sin actually resides in the law. That is the state of equilibrium. There is no balance without opposing forces. Disorder exists because of order. The moment God created order, disorder was waiting in the wings to be invoked by whomever at any time. The moment God created a hierarchy, the potential to disturb it became active. Lucifer did not invent or create sin. God did. Lucifer is not a creator: he just utilised something that already existed. If ever he did.

To credit Satan as the creator of sin is to make him equal to God because he would have created something which God did not. That would make both of them absolute or primary creators. The prime movers. The truth is that there is only one absolute or primary creator – and that is God. The rest of us are just secondary creators because we manipulate what is already there in order to make our own inventions. Lucifer did not invent sin; it was already available. Rather he simply invoked it. If ever that happened.

If Lucifer were to fight God in real terms, as others claim, he would need to be a prime mover on par with God. He would need to use weapons which God does not have control over. How can one go to war with an enemy and at the same time supply the said enemy with weapons? For now, all things that are in our universe were created by God and are sustained by God, including Lucifer and sin. In other words, Lucifer has no arsenal to fight with. The life he has is God's life. As such, he could not, cannot, and will not be able to wage war against God. Impossible. It can only be an imaginary war. Unless of course if it is fictitious – the stuff fables and legends are made of.

The so-called war between God and Satan is either an outright lie or a misconception. God cannot fight himself. Otherwise he would be just a simulator. Evil plus good equals God. Negative plus positive equals life. Evil and good are not fighting; rather, they are balancing. They seek to provide equilibrium. They find meaning in each other. Together they express and define life. Ultimately, they define God. Without evil, there is no good. Without good, there is no evil. Both evil and good exist together in God. It is a holy matrimony. They are inseparable sides of the same coin. They are husband and wife, and thus they create life.

Whatever happens in the universe, man is free to choose what to call it and how to experience it. People can decide to call anything either good or evil, either a blessing or a curse. That is the divine gift of freedom – the essence of choice. That is the ultimate gift of freedom of opinion. That is the gift of self-determination. That is why nations make constitutions. They define their good and their evil. It is their decision, and they choose to experience it as such. Each nation enacts laws to define its sins. It is a perpetual cycle. That is the beauty of life.

When you are able to view and experience the harmony between evil and good together, you can see the perfection of life. That is the perfection of God. You will enjoy every moment of it. You will take responsibility for your actions and not blame the devil nor credit it to God. You will have been saved from the illusion of heaven and hell as separate places. You will realize that you do not need to go to heaven nor to hell because they are there where you are, right inside of you – if you decide. You can then give others heaven every day if you choose, or you may give them hell any day if you decide. It is entirely up to you. You will not be judged for it; you simply reap what you sow. What you send around comes back to you. How you want to experience it is also entirely up to you. Humanity's experiences today are a function of our choices and not of God's judgements.

Therefore, the law and sin are inseparable. They are both God's creations. The so-called original heaven was already sinful because it was lawful. The only place which can be truly sinless is a lawless and orderless place. So a sinless heaven is just an illusion as long as there is order in that heaven. If, on the other hand, heaven has no governing laws, then it is a lawless place and therefore sinless. Such a place with no control, I presume, cannot be desirable.

Of course, judging by what we are witnessing today, it would seem that humanity yearns for a lawless society. Humans want to have rights to do anything. Maybe one day we will succeed in removing all the laws that are preventing us from entering the heaven we so desire. A lawless, orderless, and thus sinless society. Good luck, humanity.

As we now live in the so-called information age, we need to get rid of things inherited from what I would call the misinformation age. We cannot afford to continue to pass-on wrong information to future generations. Rather than, as is claimed, God exhuming and resurrecting humans long dead just to punish them, I foresee our great grandchildren exhuming our skeletons just to kick at them in frustration. They will be frustrated by our lack of spine to challenge uninformed perceptions of what things are and how they work. They will judge us harshly. History will condemn us for taking folklore as history, for taking the Bible as the word of God, wholesale. They will find this totally inexcusable and almost unforgivable. They will feel betrayed.

Now let us address the question of who told the truth in the forbidden tree narrative, God or Satan?

From the information available, the serpent told the complete truth, and God told an outright lie. The truth sets one free for sure because the devil is basically calm thereafter. On the other hand, it is God who is frantically trying to save himself. His plan to deceive has just spectacularly failed, and he is now facing the real 'danger' of having another God like himself who is immortal and also knows good and evil.

At this juncture, I would like to pose a question to the reader: What is your intuition saying about this story so far? Most importantly, what are the story's insinuations regarding the character and attributes of God? Would you say it is a historical event or a legendary fable?

I suppose you already know my verdict on that one. It's an emphatic 'Folklore!'

The story of the fall of man and the subsequent punishment meted out by God provide the need to examine two more important concepts – punishment and forgiveness.

Let us scrutinise how God acts relative to these two important concepts and the implications to his character.

CHAPTER 6

PUNISHMENT AND FORGIVENESS

With humans, every action provokes at least two reactions. One reaction comes from the realm of natural law and principles, and the other comes from fellow creatures, particularly other humans.

For example, if you drive recklessly and ram into the back of the car in front of you, these two reactions are triggered. First, the vehicles get damaged because of the physical forces involved on impact. Second, the other driver will confront you in response. The driver may decide to take the law into his or her own hands and give you a good hiding, or the driver may let the state decide what to do with you in accordance with the laws of the land.

The damage to the vehicles is classified as a natural consequence of the accident and is controlled by natural laws. You cannot choose the extent of the damage. On the other hand, the beating you may get from the offended driver is not naturally linked to the accident but rather is retribution for your recklessness and is administered at the discretion of the aggrieved party. This form of punishment is regarded as revenge because it is not authorised by law. But if the offended person reports you to the authorities and the said authorities send you to jail, make you pay a fine, or even cane you in some parts of the world, it is called punishment because it was administered by the authorities. Again, they use their discretion to determine the severity of the punishment.

Punishments differ in their degree of severity and may include reprimands, deprivation of privileges or liberty, fines, incarceration, ostracism, the infliction of pain, amputation, and death. We are not going to split hairs and go into detail about the various types of punishment. Rather, for the purposes of this discussion, we will just stick to the basic principle that punishment is pain (either physical or emotional) induced by a third party at their discretion and is a function of their reactive choice, whereas a natural consequence is a function of nature's reaction.

Since punishment is a function of the offended authority's choice, it may be waived by the authority through clemency. That means the offended party can choose not to punish or may choose not to be paid restitution. This waiver of punishment and restitution is called forgiveness. The offender is then technically regarded as not having erred or sinned, and the parties are said to have reconciled.

On the other hand, the natural law does not forgive, neither does it punish. It just produces the natural consequence of the action. You may sustain injuries from broken glass in the above accident, not as punishment,

This is clear retribution with no restorative benefit to God. The punishment is just meant to inflict pain on the serpent, and its suffering is seen as a desired goal in itself, even though it has no rehabilitative benefits for the offender.

The ever lingering question is, how does this 'punishment' solve the problem of sin? The crawling of the snake on the belly, the enmity with the woman and her kind, the suffering of the woman during labour, the returning of man to dust, and all the other curses pronounced by God that day – how do they resolve sin?

Certainly one would expect that this pain would have something to do with atoning for the offence committed or at least appeasing the 'offended God', but this does not seem to be the case. We are told later on that God will not accept anything except blood to atone for this sin. But he never mentioned that to the offenders in Eden. So who introduced this idea of a blood atonement for sin? The first time we find blood as part of an agreement is when God makes a covenant with Abram, but this has nothing to do with atoning for the sin in Eden. One also wonders who brought about the illusion of mankind's famous separation from God?

To what benefit did God introduce all this pain and suffering to his creatures if it did not pacify him? The measures he took are not in the category of natural consequences: This was punishment. As we noted before, punishment is pain induced on the offender to get a certain feeling of compensation or appeasement. We are not sure if that is what the God of the Bible intended to get.

Another important observation is that if God's inherent character is to forgive, then one would expect that at the very first instance of being offended he would have forgiven. He should have simply said, 'Adam, Eve, and the serpent, your sins are forgiven you. Please go and sin no more.' But he did not. Instead he was ruthless in his response. Vitriol came out of his mouth, flowing from his heart. He pronounced curses and punishments in a harsh tone. Remember, one cannot punish first and forgive later. No. Either you punish or you forgive. He could not forgive, and he has not forgiven ever since because the punishment he meted out is still active and being felt even today.

The cross of Calvary, which for millennia has stood as a symbol of forgiveness, ironically stands as the most vivid symbol of God's *unforgiveness*. When you see the cross today, it should be a reminder to you that God was so unwilling to forgive that even his so-called 'only son' had to die. The cross reinforces that God will never forgive sin; it has to be paid for. But, if one insists on restitution, he cannot claim forgiveness. In like manner, if one executes a punishment, she cannot turn around and claim willingness to forgive. Let us even be generous and say that she has decided to forgive midway through the execution of the punishment. In that case the punishment must be discontinued for forgiveness to take effect. Punishment and forgiveness cannot exist simultaneously.

Humanity is presently suffering as punishment for sin and not as a natural consequence of sin. If you look in any direction, you see a cross, and this cross is meant to tell you that all your sins have been paid for. Please note: paid for – not forgiven. However, you are told that you cannot access the relief unless you believe that Jesus died record of wrongs. But here is God with a long, accurate list of all wrongs. Every wrong word, thought, deed, everything. There is a book of life, a book of remembrance, and a book of death, and names are constantly being moved from one book to the other depending on what you do moment by moment. God using books and being so vindictive? What are we saying to ourselves? Surely we need to wake up from this slumber. The sooner we do so, the better.

What is of critical importance regarding punishment is that, since the offended party (or representative authority) determines the nature and degree of the punishment, he should be appeased by it. In this case, God determined the punishment he felt was commensurate with the offence in the Garden of Eden and meted it out. He never mentioned that he would like them to shed their blood to be reconciled with him. He just unrolled a long list of curses as punishment. No forgiveness. Done and dusted. Just like any father who takes his son shopping soon after spanking him for a misdeed, God goes on to make clothes for his children immediately thereafter, and the communion carries on. There is no separation at all except that man is barred from accessing the tree of life. Neither Adam nor Eve appear to be alienated from God.

Therefore, the belated talk of God having a plan of salvation and forgiveness through the shedding of blood becomes a total fabrication. Forgiveness for which sin? The same sin that mankind has received punishment for? Even then, the so-called plan of salvation reinforces the fact that God is unwilling to forgive sin. It must be paid for at all cost. Someone must die to pay for the sin. If a debt is paid up in full, what is there to write off? By insisting on payment, God has ruled out forgiveness, even if he pays from his own pocket, as it were. The principle here is that nothing comes for free. Sin cannot go unpunished. Worse still, sin cannot be forgiven.

Let us be generous and say that Jesus of Nazareth died to atone for sin. Then the raw fact is still that the sins were paid for and nothing was forgiven. What do we say then about all the suffering by humanity and the rest of creation purportedly because of the curses pronounced as punishment by God? What purpose does this pain serve? This simply achieves one thing: to portray God as one whose wrath is unquenchable. He is so obsessed with vengeance that he will actually resurrect sinners just to burn them in hell. All he wants is to fix them and make them suffer excruciating pain while he probably enjoys it. He will even keep sustaining their lives in order for them to burn for eternity. Just imagine a God with such a mentality. Surely God, the Supreme Being, cannot do such a subhuman thing as this.

In short, what we see here is that the natural consequence of their actions was that their eyes were opened and they became like God to know good and evil. It was not God who opened their eyes; the fruit did. All the other things were actions of a third party, God, whose appetite for cursing seems unquenchable. He banished them from the garden, deprived them of the tree of life, and added all the curses as punishment, as if embarrassed that they did not die as he had prophesied. I do not think God would ever stoop so low.

so on, I honestly don't think they were designed to eat grass.

It is one of two things: either God designed all his creatures once and for all, or he had to redesign all of them after the 'fall of man' in order to facilitate the implementation of his curses. That would mean changing all the digestive systems of all the different species and in many cases creating extra features such as fangs, paws, incisors, claws, and beaks. So God had to redesign the ecosystem so that his curses could be applied. That would be effectively adding to the original creation week. This surely must be taken with serious doubts.

The main reason for all this is allegedly because God could not forgive. We are all encouraged to forgive one another unconditionally for at least seventy times seven times – that is, if we can be unloving enough to keep a record. We are admonished to love our enemies and to bless those that persecute us. But God himself cannot forgive Lucifer. If Lucifer caused the fall of man, then he should be the first one to be forgiven because he was the first offender. If God cannot forgive Lucifer, then he must just keep quiet about forgiveness. He is not a good example of a forgiver. If God cannot forgive his enemy, Lucifer, how does he expect us to forgive our enemies? He must lead by example.

That takes us to another legend, the story of creation itself. Let us look at it through the microscope.

CHAPTER 7

THE STORY OF CREATION

To a gullible, innocent soul, the story of creation as given in the Genesis narrative appears to be sound doctrine based on a true historical event. However, a closer look at the detail reveals something totally different. The storyline is unmistakably consistent with legendary storytelling. It clearly reveals the misconceptions held by the author(s) about the universe. At face value, the two chapters (Genesis 1–2) seem to be complimentary, but a closer analysis clearly reflects otherwise. The two chapters are actually in conflict and probably originate from two different legendary stories. Both versions have characteristics of legends. They seem to be more folklore than history.

The version of creation found in the chapter of Genesis 1 and up to the first three verses of chapter 2 seem to give a chronological sequence of the creation story. But Genesis 2: 4–23 gives a different version of the creation account. The version of chapter 2 is disjointed and has no time frames. It appears to be a reckless attempt to lay the foundation for the fall of man, which is then told in chapter 3. Chapter 2 introduces a number of things that are not captured in chapter 1:

- the planting of the Garden of Eden
- the creation of man from soil
- the placing of the man in the Garden of Eden
- the creation of a woman from a man's rib
- the tree of life and the tree of knowledge
- the command not to eat fruit from the tree of knowledge
- the concept of death
- the need for watering the earth before plants could grow

The author of Genesis 2 seems to imply that man was created before the plants, whereas Genesis 1 says the plants were made on the third day and man on the sixth. The author of Genesis 2 seems also to say that God, after realising that man was lonely, brought animals to the man in an effort to get a suitable helper for him, in addition to having him name them. After failing to find a suitable helper for man among the animals, God is said to have used one of the man's ribs to make a woman. But Genesis 1 simply says he created them male and female and commanded them to be fruitful and multiply on the sixth day.

The author of Genesis 2 further implies that there were no plants at first simply because God had not sent rain, so the ground would be watered by rivers underneath. But Genesis 1 had no need to water the earth because it was already wet since the plants were created on the same third day that God moved the waters to seas to expose dry land. Surely the ground still had enough moisture to sustain plant life.

It is the author of Genesis 2 who introduces the idea of a tree of life and another one for knowing good and evil. He also introduces the command not to eat from the tree of knowledge, along with the concept of disobedience and death, regardless of the fact that, at that point, mankind had no capacity to understand these ideas.

It seems the idea was just to create a foundation for the so-called fall from grace and the subsequent illusion of separation from God: the two major concepts that would later give birth to the grand idea of a salvation plan.

One major characteristic of legendary folklore is that it develops stories in retrospect. It uses existing facts to speculate and attempt to establish the origins of natural phenomena. At its best, folklore is simply creative speculation meant to fill the void created by lack of knowledge.

The very mention of names such as Cush, Havilah, Euphrates, and other contemporary names indicates how long after the narrative of chapter 1 that Genesis 2 was written. Chapter 2 is then concluded by typical legendary statements: [24] 'That is why a man leaves his father and mother and is united to his wife, and they become one flesh. [25] Adam and his wife were both naked, and they felt no shame.'

Folklore is always concluded by such statements like 'that is why an eagle eats chicks' or 'that is how the tortoise got his chequered shell' or 'that is why a man leaves his parents'. Their essential purpose is to speculate about how things as they are now could have begun. They are always written in retrospect. That was the work of our gifted storytellers.

In actual fact, there is nothing wrong with legends and fables, as long as they are labelled as such. The only problem is in labelling folklore as true history. Worse still is to label it as 'the word of God' and teach it as history to successive generations. That is criminal.

Let us examine a few themes in the narrative of the story of creation and see if they can be validated by Mother Nature to be facts of history or legendary storytelling. It is important to emphasise at this juncture that, for an event to be classified as history, it must have happened in the realm of space and time. In other words, history is literal in terms of occurrence. It is not a function of imagination; rather, it is a function of observation and actual experience.

Let us start with Genesis 1: 1–5, the purported events of the first day of creation:

> [1]In the beginning God created the heavens and the earth. [2]Now the earth was formless and empty, darkness was over the surface of the deep, and the Spirit of God was hovering over the waters.
>
> [3]And God said, 'Let there be light,' and there was light. [4]God saw that the light was good, and he separated the light from the darkness. [5]God called the light 'day,' and the darkness he

called 'night'. And there was evening, and there
was morning—the first day.

According to the narrative, only God and darkness
existed before the first day of creation. Nothing else had
been made, and God only started on this particular 'day'
to exercise his creative powers. From eternity past up
until that moment, God was part of a great darkness.
No problem. I suppose God does not need light for him
to exist. One thing that would seem to be clear, though,
is that God did not create darkness. He is a part of it. It
was already there with him because darkness is simply the
absence of light. Light was only created on the magical
first day.

In the meantime, let us hold on to the assumption
that the author(s) of this narrative are receiving the
information they are writing from God; more aptly, God
is writing through them, as is claimed.

So in that great darkness, God makes the heavens, the
earth, and water. Bang! This seems to concur with the Big
Bang theory because it happens in a short span of time:
less than a day, to be precise. The 'heavens' in this case
probably mean the rest of the universe and all its galaxies
as we know them now but excluding the earth. There is
a clear, deliberate narrowing of focus to the earth and to
present it as separate from the heavens.

The author then claims that the earth was formless
and was covered by a lot of water, on top of which the
spirit of God hovered. But we now know that the earth is
a sphere. It would seem that the author of Genesis at the
time of writing did not know that the earth was spherical.
Obviously God knew that the earth had form and was

a sphere. This then raised the question: Is the idea of a formless earth coming from God or from the mind of the writer? I don't think God would have ever said, or caused to be said, that the earth was formless. This is a classic example of the limitedness of human imagination. This is creative speculation.

After this kind of 'big bang', God is said to have then concentrated on the earth and what we now know as our solar system for the rest of the creation week. In short, it is implied that God created the entire universe and an empty earth in the first few moments of the first day of creation, except for things that are in our solar system and earthly life. The rest of that first day and the remainder of the creation week were dedicated solely to creative work on planet Earth and our solar system.

To wind up the first day, God is said to have created light and then separated light from darkness to create day and night. There is no specified source of this light. It is just light. The narrative even implies that this light was *not* radiating from God himself if God existed in the great darkness all along and there was no light. He probably created a source of light, which he could manipulate to have the day and night experience.

Before this first 'day' of creation, there was no light, although God was there. And this newly created light could somehow be separated from darkness to mark day and night. This cycle carries on until the fourth day, when the sun, the moon, and the stars are said to be then made, supposedly to provide light during day and night respectively. But we now know that the experience of alternating day and night is an effect of Earth revolving about its axis as it orbits the sun. Light is permanently radiating from the sun. Night is only experienced on the shadow side of Earth, and the position of this shadow is constantly changing as Earth rotates, The sun then seems to be moving. There is no universal night in the sky because the sun is always shining. This information was not known by the author. And the author is supposed to be God?

Having day and night for four days before the sun was made seems to be a simple fabrication. The very idea that the earth was created before the sun is inaccurate. We now know that earthly plant life depends on the sun in the same way that day and night depends on the sun. Therefore, for an orderly God to have created these before the sun is very unlikely. The idea that the sun was created four days after the earth is fuelled by the misconception that the earth is the biggest body in the universe, which we now know to be false. If all these bodies were not created at the same time, then it is mostly likely that the sun was created first, by virtue of being the centre and mainstay of our solar system.

Even more revealing about the author's misconceptions is the seeming existence of a universal day and night on earth, as if the entire earth experiences day at the same time. Now we know that the earth experiences both night and day simultaneously. Half of the earth is in darkness, and the other half is lit at any given time, and this is constantly shifting as the planet rotates on its axis. Therefore, the experience of day or night becomes a function of one's location. As a result, it is entirely possible for people to permanently experience day or night if they can move along the surface of the earth at exactly the same speed as the earth's circumferential speed relative to their location. At the equator, for example, it will be about 1670 km/hr. I know that some might argue that this is scientific knowledge, but we must remember that scientists do not create principles; they only discover them through study and observation driven by inspiration. It is important to realise that religion does not hold a monopoly on divine inspiration. Scientific discovery is also by divine inspiration.

God cannot inspire factual error. It is clear that the author had grave misconceptions about what causes the earthly experience of day and night. Certainly that author cannot be God the creator himself, or even claim to have been 'inspired' by God to write such inaccurate information.

The misconception at the time was that Earth was the centre of the universe (geocentrism) and that it was flat and fixed while everything else could move. Earth was thought to be the biggest body in the universe, and all other bodies could actually fall and fit on the surface of it. That is to say, the sun, moon, and all the stars, if they were to fall, could fit on Earth's surface and were small enough for humans to move around and possibly pick up. It was also thought in many cultures to be possible for humans to build a tall enough structure to collect these stars. There was no accurate sense of distance in those days. Distance and the size of the stars was a huge misconception. The author therefore thought that the moon was bigger than all the stars and that its sole purpose was to provide light during the night. We now know that this is not correct.

Some stars are many times bigger than our sun. Certainly the author could not have been God.

Just to put this in perspective, as recently as the early seventeenth century, Galileo Galilei, 'the father of modern physics', was persecuted and had to spend the last part of his life under house arrest for concurring with Nicholas Copernicus' theory of heliocentrism. This discovery revealed that the sun was in fact the biggest body in our solar system and lay in the centre while Earth and the other planets orbit it.

The irony of all ironies is that it was the church that condemned Galileo for being a heretic. Therefore, it is clear that God had not revealed to the church how the universe works – not even the 'wise men from the east'. Not even Jesus himself attempted to do it. Although many people and even Catholic schools were teaching heliocentrism long before 1992, it took the church until very late in the twentieth century (1992) to issue a formal apology through Pope John Paul II for Galileo's condemnation and treatment. We should salute the courage, sincerity, and bravery of Pope John Paul II to accept that the church was wrong. That indeed is the silver lining of the dark cloud. Probably for this reason more than anything else he deserves to be a saint.

Surely God could not have 'inspired' the church to err all along, only to be corrected by science and astronomy thousands of years later. The narrative was clearly not written by God. It can only be legendary, not historical.

Consider the following from Wikipedia:

> Biblical references sometimes used to attack
> heliocentrism included Psalm 93:1, 96:10, and

1 Chronicles 16:30 include text stating that "the world is firmly established, it cannot be moved." In the same manner, Psalm 104:5 says, "The Lord set the earth on its foundations; it can never be moved." Further, Ecclesiastes 1:5 states that "And the sun rises and sets and returns to its place." Galileo defended heliocentrism, and in his Letter to the Grand Duchess Christina argued that it was not contrary to biblical texts. He took the Augustinian position that poetry, songs, instructions or historical statements in biblical texts need not always be interpreted literally. Galileo argued that the authors wrote from the perspective of the terrestrial world in which the sun does rise and set, and discussed a different kind of "movement" of the earth, not rotations.

By 1615 Galileo's writings on heliocentrism had been submitted to the Roman Inquisition, though his greater offense was his attempt to reinterpret the Bible, which was seen as a violation of the Council of Trent and looked dangerously like Protestantism. Galileo went to Rome to defend himself and his Copernican and biblical idea.

In March 2008 the head of the Pontifical Academy of Sciences, Nicola Cabibbo, announced a plan to honour Galileo by erecting a statue of him inside the Vatican walls. In December of the same year, during events to mark the 400th anniversary of Galileo's earliest telescopic observations, Pope Benedict XVI praised his contributions to astronomy. A month later, however, the head of the

Pontifical Council for Culture, Gianfranco Ravasi, revealed that the plan to erect a statue of Galileo in the grounds of the Vatican had been suspended.

Context is always the key. We can see here the great danger of taking legends, poetry, songs, instructions, or historical statements literally and labelling them 'word of God' without recognising the presence of the author's misconceptions. It is a dangerous trap which can easily lead to rigid indoctrination.

The misconception (geocentrism) carries on into the second day of creation when the author describes the creation of the sky, the seas, and the plants. The writer actually insinuates that the blue sky we see above us is a massive body of water. He narrates how God separated the waters into two bodies: one that remained covering the earth and the other that was moved up to create the space called firmament, or heaven or sky. The water that remained below was moved over to create the seas, and the dry earth appeared. Then the plants were made and so on.

The most absurd claim could be that there is a huge body of water way beyond the stars in our solar system but below the heavens (galaxies). We now know that the blue sky is not a massive body of water. We can see (even with the naked eye) things way beyond our solar system. We surely would not see that through a massive body of water. We already know of more than a hundred billion galaxies discovered hundreds of millions of light years from Earth. One light year is approximately 9 trillion kilometres (or about 6 trillion miles).

The question now is, who is inspired – the scientist or the speculative author of Genesis? All hail God through the scientist. The great irony is that the scientist does not claim inspiration although he clearly has it, and the speculative author who claims inspiration clearly does not have it.

Sir Isaac Newton, the great British scientist, removed the last doubts about the validity of the heliocentric model of the solar system. His *Principia* describing the laws of motion and universal gravitation would dominate scientists' view of the physical universe for the next three centuries. By deriving Kepler's laws of planetary motion from his mathematical description of gravity, and then using the same principles to account for the trajectories of comets, the tides, the precession of the equinoxes, and other phenomena, he removed all doubts about heliocentrism.

It seems crystal clear to a sincere mind whose common sense is enabled that the creation narrative of Genesis is factually incorrect and is based on human misconceptions about how nature works. Crucially, because of the inherent inaccuracies, it cannot and should not be attributed to God. Therefore the narrative must be labelled correctly as a legendary story.

It is probably this huge misconception about the size and position of the earth that led to the idea that God is desirous of establishing a kingdom on earth and reigning here forever. This is the central idea taught through the ages by the Bible and its off-shoot religions.

God is the creator. He does not need a kingdom. He has no rival on earth nor in the universe. To claim that

God wants to establish a kingdom is to reduce him to the level of his creation. God is like the ocean. You cannot compare the sea with dams and rivers. It is the source of all the water in the rivers. It would be crazy to say the sea wants to come to the land to establish a river that is better than all rivers. It is equally crazy to suggest that God wants to set up a kingdom on earth. It is like a school headmaster who wants to make himself head boy. Like a country's president contesting a mayoral election in one of the country's cities.

It is actually worse than that. I fail to find a proper illustration to show the gulf between God the Supreme Being and a king. Kingdoms are for humans because they have territories with boundaries. Who knows the boundaries of the universe? God is not the King of Kings. He is the owner of kings. A headmaster *is not* the prefect of prefects. He is the head of the school, with or without prefects. If God were to set up a kingdom on earth, that would make him very small indeed. Then what would happen to the rest of the cosmos if God were to be stationed on earth? Just imagine. The problem is not with God; it is with humanity's misconceptions about how things work. It is about humanity's limited knowledge, which manifests as the so-called fundamental beliefs. Not fundamental knowledge.

If God were to set up an earthly kingdom, surely that would be the greatest demotion of all time. God is the creator. He is the all-in-all. He owns everything, whereas a king has dominion over a given territory but does not own it. God is the owner and is not needy.

This idea of a God who will establish an earthly kingdom has been around for millennia. The Christians accuse the Jews of failing to recognise Jesus of Nazareth as the messiah because they say Jews mistakenly expected a messiah to set up an earthly kingdom, but many Christians still have the same expectation. They are waiting for a Jesus of Nazareth who will return to establish an everlasting earthly kingdom of God. The only difference is that he will take them first to a 'honeymoon' for a thousand years somewhere in a place called 'heaven', wherever that is. After that he will come back to earth to establish an earthly kingdom forever, and God will be based on earth. How they hope to count years in heaven where there is no sun to create night and day is not clear. They claim that there will be no need for the sun because God himself will be the light. This further shows the misconception they have about the purpose of the sun. They seem to forget that the sun actually supports plant life on earth apart from giving light.

It is said that there will be a cubical city whose length, width, and height are equal to 2400 km (12,000 furlongs, i.e. 2,400 kilometres). A furlong is approximately 200 metres. One can understand the width and breath, but for a city to be 2400 km tall is stretching it. It just boggles the mind. The city will be surrounded by a wall approximately 66 metres high with twelve gates and twelve foundations representing the twelve tribes of Israel and the twelve apostles respectively. The city is 2400 km high, but the perimeter wall is a mere 66 metres in height. What purpose that wall with gates serves in a sinless society, nobody knows. The notion of a God based with humans in a city is the clearest evidence of humanity's misconceptions about God and the universe. It certainly would qualify as childish imagination.

Effectively, the earth would become the centre of the universe once again (geocentrism). They claim that in the new earth, there will be no sea; the sun will not shine again; there will be no death, pain, or – most bizarrely – no sin, as if in a lawless society. All of these things simply seem to be human wishes based on two great misconceptions: one about God and the other about the universe. Why would God want a wall and gates around the city? We are told because outside the city there are dogs and witches. Why would God do away with the sea and the sun as if they were sinful?

I hope I will not be stretching the truth if I suggest that the one who wanted the sea removed was John the author of Revelation because he was detained on the island of Patmos. The sea stood between him and freedom, so he probably longed for an earth without the sea. With all due respect, John seems to be hallucinating; therefore, for humans to entrust our entire future on John's assertions surely borders on recklessness.

The list of John's and other authors' claims about heaven is long, but the central theme is that humanity does not want to take responsibility for anything anymore. They want their freedom of choice to be revoked on the so-called 'new earth'. There humans must be changed and will be controlled by instinct, not choice. They must be 'slaves of righteousness'. No more conscience, only instinct. And God is said to be supremely happy with the new setup. How sad.

God is the creator of everything. Being the creator is the greatest title one can ever have. For God to desire to be a king is just inconceivable. For God to have a kingdom, there must be another kingdom(s) to rival his. That is why he is thought to be at war with his creature, Satan, who happens to have a kingdom of his own too. The idea borders on insulting God. This is an illusion that must be discarded, while humanity must wake up now to take full responsibility for its actions. It must stop attributing its actions to the influence of the two kingdoms that humans themselves have created. There is only one God, no rival. The rest is his creation. The idea of a rival God and an ongoing war is probably mankind's most poisonous invention. It is a weapon of mass destruction. It must be discarded together with nuclear weapons.

One important lesson we learn from the church's apology to Galileo is that scientific and religious claims should be regarded as complementary, not separate. If something is not yet proven beyond doubt, then belief can temporarily hold sway. But if there is empirical evidence, then science must prevail. We should not hold on to speculative belief after receiving true knowledge.

In the next chapter, we will examine these two concepts, belief and knowledge.

CHAPTER 8

BELIEF VERSUS KNOWLEDGE

People are often asked to just believe in order to be saved. They even get referred to as 'believers'. People's beliefs are protected fiercely, to the point of being included in national constitutions, but just what is this magical concept called belief?

According to the Oxford Dictionary, 'belief is the state of mind in which a person thinks something to be the case, with or without there being empirical evidence to prove that something is the case with factual certainty. In other words, belief is when someone thinks something is reality, true, when they have no absolute verified foundation for their certainty of the truth or realness of something'.

According to the *Stanford Encyclopaedia of Philosophy*, belief is 'a mental representation of an attitude positively orientated towards the likelihood of something being true'.

The major take-home point for me is that belief is not conclusive and lacks certainty. Therefore, there is always the possibility of it changing with improved visibility. It simply provides a starting point on the journey of discovery. The ultimate destination is absolute knowledge. Therefore, in that regard, belief is some form of ignorance.

Perhaps belief is one of the most misunderstood and misused concepts in the world today. Belief is a function of wishful thinking and not a function of knowledge. True knowledge is a function of discovery and experience. A belief is more perception than principle because it is subjective. It is based on hope and not truth. It is more like an emotional preference. It is to accept something as truth without knowledge.

To me, belief is a subtle form of ignorance, a dim form of darkness. Here is why: belief only works in the absence of absolute knowledge. It is a precursor to knowledge, at best. Belief is kind of forerunner but is not the real deal. It always has an undercurrent of uncertainty. But all this is suppressed by wishful thinking disguised as hope. This false hope creates a counterfeit form of faith, which leads to reckless gullibility.

Belief is a slight improvement on ignorance but is a form of ignorance nonetheless. When knowledge arrives, belief disappears.

The cardinal rule is this: You cannot believe in something that you know. You can only believe in something that you do *not* know. Knowledge is a higher virtue than belief.

A doctrine is a belief. It is not inherently true. It is not knowledge. It is a perception that is declared to be truth and taught as if it were a genuine principle. A belief should have a temporary lifespan, but knowledge is eternal. It is also important to note that sometimes belief is a necessary step towards knowledge. However, belief *must*, I repeat *must*, give way to knowledge eventually.

Once knowledge appears, belief cannot return again. Belief, in its purest form, is half-truth. There is always a possibility that it might change. However, once absolute knowledge arrives, belief disappears.

Knowledge is synonymous with light and allows us to see clearly. We cannot have full light and total darkness in the same space at the same time. If we know, then we do not need to believe, but if we believe, we will need to know at some stage.

One prophet Hosea once said, 'My people perish because of lack of knowledge'. He did not say they died because of lack of belief.

Admittedly, belief occupies a very important place in human life, but even in its purest form, it is only a precursor to knowledge. The tricky part is that to most people, belief is synonymous with knowledge. However, subconsciously they are aware that the belief might not be absolute truth. As a result, the fear of being wrong activates a natural defence system led by emotional insecurity. They cleverly insinuate that any attack on the belief's authenticity is an attack on their person. A firewall is built around the belief, and emotions quickly kick in. The belief is therefore defended with anger and intolerance.

Subsequently, claims are made to the effect that the belief is absolute truth and cannot be questioned nor even improved upon. Henceforth, anyone with a contrary opinion is labelled an enemy, given the derogatory name of 'gentile', and thus can be killed without regret and with

God's approval. Thus the half-truth is sealed as absolute knowledge and must be taught as divine doctrine. A religion is born. The battle for minds begins, and perception formulation replaces genuine love and integrity. The next generation of believers is born, who must also believe with fear and trembling. What a tragedy.

Belief comprises two parts, which are progressively linked. These are 'belief about' and 'belief in' something. There is a distinct difference between the two, and 'belief about' comes first. Belief about something relates to the perceived characteristics of the relevant object, such as its shape, form, strength, intellect, emotions, authority, character, influence, and so on. On the other hand, 'belief in' something is based on your relationship with that object and has to do with its perceived performance capabilities for you. It feeds directly from your 'belief about' it. If the 'belief about' does not mature to 'knowledge about', one is said to be deluded. This leads to disappointment because the performance level will not match the expectation.

Let us use some analogies to simplify the matter. It is almost every child's belief 'about' a father that he is the most powerful person on earth. As a result, children believe in their fathers' ability to conquer every other father on earth. If, for example, your belief about God is that he has a body with human features and sits on a throne somewhere, then you can perceive (believe in) him leaving the throne and 'coming' to another place to interact with humans or animals.

You will notice that all deception is ultimately based on a corrupted 'belief about' something. If you can corrupt what someone believes *about* something, then you have corrupted what they believe *in*. Fortunately, knowledge is incorruptible. Only belief can be corrupted.

Our greatest challenge, which is also the present need for humanity, is to graduate from belief to knowledge. Most of the bloodshed in the world today may be traced back to a corrupted belief.

It is important to realise that belief about something does not change the object in absolute terms. The object remains what it is regardless of what you believe about it. Belief is a function of your perception, but knowledge is a function of discovery. That is why beliefs are associated with high emotions. Questioning a belief is regarded as an attack on the believer, so the believer feels obliged to defend the belief, even if it means killing for it. Truth needs no defence, but belief must be defended. Truth is God and God cannot be defended by man. God defends man and sets him free. The truth sets you free; you do not set the truth free.

As an example, suppose you pick up a stone in your garden that has some shiny yellow particles imbedded in it. You may decide to believe that it has gold in it until you conduct tests that confirm it or disprove it. Then you will have discovered the truth. Knowledge is truth discovered or revealed, and it does not change, whereas belief is truth covered or concealed, and it can change.

If your religion is made up of a long list of the so-called fundamental beliefs, that should be a red flag to you. These beliefs must become fundamental knowledge eventually. You must seek to *know* all those beliefs. Discover, or better still, un-cover the truth. Don't be afraid. Question them, study them, and discover the truth about them. Be knowledgeable; don't just believe. Remember this: belief is not truth to you until it becomes knowledge. Believing does not convert a misconception into truth. Likewise, a doctrine is not necessarily a truth. It is merely a belief waiting to be confirmed as truth or as falsehood. It is your duty to discover the truth. This is the duty of humanity. Do not delegate this job to someone else.

Belief about something must mature into knowledge about it. Knowledge then breeds 'trust in' that thing. It is trust which breeds faith. In the end, faith and trust become interchangeable. One cannot have faith in someone or something one does not know. That is recklessness, to put it mildly. Knowledge comes first, then trust and then faith.

Take the famous story of Abraham being instructed to sacrifice his son Isaac. He absolutely knew the source of the instruction. He did not *believe* that God gave him the instruction. He *knew* that it was God who gave the instruction. He knew him from previous encounters, and this knowledge had led him to develop trust in God. Because of the trust he had in the source of the instruction, he executed it in faith (hope based on knowledge). So the maturity continuum looks something like this: belief – knowledge – trust – faith. Abraham had knowledge of God. He had passed the stage of believing in God. This knowledge about God informed his trust in God; therefore, he could act in faith. Faith is always acted upon. If faith does not result in action, it is useless. However, faith is not blind. It is not wishful thinking. It is driven by the hope that the relationship we have will influence the other party to act. It is based on trust in, and knowledge of, the driving force.

The fatal mistake most humans make is assuming that belief equates to knowledge. Hence they jump from belief straight into trust and faith. Some even jump from belief to faith – the tragic result being either disappointment or radicalization. Imagine the disappointment of discovering that your wife was raped by someone you 'believed' was a prophet. Ever heard of the 1844 Great Disappointment? The cause was jumping from belief straight to faith. The problem with faith is that it is kind of a verb. It is an action word. You cannot have faith without acting upon it. There is no dormant faith. Faith without knowledge is pure recklessness.

When one acts from belief alone, one tends to become irrational, emotional, judgemental, and, ultimately, suicidal. When the belief is questioned, the believer feels attacked personally and immediately engages in self-defence. The believer is spoiling for a fight because a belief is very vulnerable by its nature. Its only line of defence is the believer.

For a belief to survive, it must be converted into a doctrine. A declaration. A mere claim. Then the believer must be indoctrinated until the belief becomes a faith. Remember, faith is action. Now, since the belief is not necessarily truth, its survival depends on the believer, and the believer must defend it. The believer becomes the God or creator, and the belief becomes the creature. Once the believer reaches the stage of owning the belief, he or she has become indoctrinated. This is a dangerous condition to be in.

The next stage is radicalization. Indoctrination and radicalization share one poisonous feature: they prohibit the use of common sense. Remember, when your common sense is disabled, you cease to be human. You become a robot, and you are doomed.

Radicalization manifests in many forms, but the most dominant form is the idea that man can please God, the Supreme Being, by acts of self-denial and sacrifice. The implementation of this idea differs from religion to religion or, more aptly, from belief system to belief system. The results are there for all to see.

It is critically important to remember that belief systems and doctrines are man-made. They are not necessarily God-given. They evolve. In the same manner in which the shadow shortens as the sun rises, so do beliefs: they disappear as knowledge increases.

The big challenge is resolving the question: How does belief graduate to become true knowledge? The answer is a threefold: nature, common sense, and intuition. Nature 'speaks' to us through natural laws. These natural laws are mankind's source of education in addition to inspiration and intuition. They are engraved on our hearts and are validated by our environment. Any claim, doctrine, or theory must therefore be validated by nature through observation. One of the unwritten natural laws that I've observed is that anything that reproduces its kind has a lifespan. It does not live forever, except in the sense that it passes life on to the next generation of its species.

Humanity falls squarely into this category of creation. Physical mankind has a lifespan. People pass all that they have on to the next generation and thus live through their offspring. That is the design. That is how God intended it to be. The physical body expires and decomposes. First it is composed when various foods and other substances come together, energised and bonded by the spiritual body. Once the spiritual body leaves, the physical body returns to its constituent elements. Energy simply changes from one form to the other. The spiritual body lives on because it is not subject to death. This is validated by nature. This is confirmed by the fact that most cultures have a way of interaction between the living and the departed loved ones.

In short, people must be very cautious when they use belief as a basis for decision making. Therefore for God to use belief in Jesus of Nazareth as the criterion for salvation, in my view, would be to reward recklessness. It is the ultimate lottery. It is like God encouraging gambling. Most people mistake a wish for a belief. If you wish for a certain outcome, you desire it but do not know whether it will come to be. Actually you have a genuine fear that it will not be so. To keep yourself positive, you hope it will turn out as you wish, but since there is no knowledge, you sustain hope by believing in it. Hope and belief then sustain each other. But belief is not knowledge. Belief is a game of chance. If you are right, you win big, and if you are wrong, you lose big as well. Ultimately, belief means taking a gamble with the given information in the hope that it turns out to be true.

Because belief is not conclusive, it should never be the basis for major decisions, especially where life-and-death issues are involved. Scepticism might actually be more valuable than belief. Being sceptical gives you the freedom to question and test. When you question and test, you stand a chance of eventually coming to a knowingness. Being sceptical has more virtue than being gullible. It might actually be more beneficial to be a 'doubting Thomas' than a reckless follower.

Lack of belief cannot and should not be regarded as sin. God cannot and will not condemn anyone for lacking belief. Before one believes in the Bible, one needs to examine his or her beliefs about the Bible. Crucially, one must examine its origin. The greatest tragedy is that the majority of us are too lazy to verify the origins of the claims about the Bible. We need some kind of fact-check, and even intelligence checks, just like what governments and large corporations do before engaging in business ventures and investments. They do not use belief where knowledge is required. How much more diligence is required with one's own life? Your beliefs about the bible must graduate to true knowledge.

I urge you to make it your top priority to verify the claims about the Bible before committing your only life to it. Study its origin. You may soon realise that the more you know about the origins of the Bible, the clearer the subject of its infallibility becomes. Go on. Do not fear. Do not remain in darkness about the Bible. Remember what Jesus of Nazareth said: 'If the light that is in you is darkness, how great is that darkness'. The surest sign you can have that you are in the dark about the Bible is to believe that it is infallible. That surely must frighten you.

Let us therefore explore the claim that the Bible is the word of God.

Chapter 9

IS THE BIBLE THE WORD OF GOD?

Although the Bible is loosely referred to as the 'word of God', it is important to note that its various categories do not carry the same weight. It would seem, from these simple categories, that not everything in the Bible is actually the word of God, as claimed by so many. Therefore, to say that the Bible in its current bound state is the word of God might just be an overzealous exaggeration.

It seems to me that the phrase 'word of God' might have been coined to give the book the status of being the mouthpiece of God, probably because of difficulties encountered in selling some of the messages. Fear of rejection made it necessary to intimidate the listeners and readers with the now famous phrase 'word of God'. This phrase, whether by conscious design or not, could also have been meant to instil fear in the reader's mind, and it has worked wonders so far, I suppose.

The underlying assumption is that God inspired the authors to reveal himself to mankind. One wonders, though: For which generation of mankind is the Bible written? Is it only for the so-called 'end time' generation? If it took 1500 years to write the Bible, what happens to those generations who lived without it and those generations that lived during its compilation? If the book is the instruction manual for life, why was it not given at the very beginning? Furthermore, it reached some parts of the world, Africa for example, only in the late nineteenth century. What is the fate of all our ancestors who never got to hear about this 'book from God'? Are they all going to hell? How will they be judged? But if there is another criterion, other than believing in Jesus, which is going to be used for them, then surely 'salvation' has nothing to do with belief in Jesus of Nazareth. The very existence of an alternative criterion nullifies the claim about salvation through belief in Jesus alone.

That the Bible is the word of God is a common statement, mostly from those who profess to be Christians. But what is the origin of this statement, and is it true and, if so, in what context? It is God's word to whom?

Religious perceptions are formed by indoctrination. Perceptions in general, or paradigms as Steven Covey would call them, 'are the lenses through which we see the world'. In absolute terms, it is not true to say the Bible is the word of God. It would seem to me to be just an emotional Christian wish expressed as reality. So who said the Bible is the word of God? Is it God himself or it is humanity? Let us examine this more by looking at the origin of the book.

How did the Bible come into being? Did it fall from the sky bound as the book it is now? Who put it together? Research shows that it was written by many authors over a period covering 1500 years. Scholars debated, agreed, and also disagreed on what eventually became the cannon, as well as whether the canon should be closed or remain open. They gathered together all the Jewish writings (scriptures) they could get. Therefore the phrase 'all scripture' in 2 Timothy 3: 16 refers to all these writings well before the exercise of canonization. Unfortunately, a lot of scriptures were left out for various reasons. One of the chief reasons was that they were regarded as not good enough for specific doctrine formulation, though possibly good for edification.

Nevertheless, they say 'all' scripture was inspired by God. So who authorised the compilers to leave out some scriptures, which then formed the Apocrypha? The book of Enoch was left out, the gospel according to Phillip was left out, the gospel according to Judas, the gospel according to Mary Magdalene was left out, and the list is long. When one reads what Phillip says about the relationship between Jesus of Nazareth and Mary Magdalene plus what Judas says about his innocence regarding selling Jesus out, one understands why some books were left out.

The bottom line is this: If the scholars wanted to compile 'all scripture', they should have just done that without discriminating. They should have left the canon open so that if other scriptures were later discovered, they could be added. The Dead Sea Scrolls are a good example. Therefore the compilers are guilty of subtracting from scripture. It is important to note that texts that are often quoted as prohibiting the addition or subtraction of scripture are not referring to the Bible in its present canon but rather to 'specific messages from God' (Deut. 4:2, Deut. 12:32, Prov. 30:5–6, Rev. 22:18–19).

Who coined the phrase "The Holy Bible" and why?

The Catholic Church did. It is important to note that the term 'holy' in this regard is supposed to be used in relative terms and is not absolute. The book is not holy to everyone, just like my mother is not a mother to all people. It is supposed to be holy to the Israelites/Jews. There should be no risk of blasphemy if a non-Israelite does not honour it except when visiting Israel. Then he or she must honour it as a matter of etiquette. It is this flexibility that is lacking or that is not emphasized. Instead, the Bible is forced down others' throats as the de facto word of God. If you do not regard it as such, hellfire and brimstone are said to be waiting to torment you for eternity. This is classic fear-mongering driven by insecurity.

I remember this fear very vividly. We were forbidden to put any other book on top of the Bible under any circumstances: not even a hymn book or a small quarterly lesson book. It was taboo. It might still be taboo to some right now.

A second phrase was introduced to cement the notion of God's involvement in the writing of the Bible. People probably thought that if God is holy and the Bible is wholly acceptable as 'the word of a holy God', then the Bible must be a holy book. This gave birth to the questionable and possibly misleading phrase, 'the holy Bible'. The Catholic Church actually coined these two phrases. The conviction could have been real, but the motive can be characterised as fear-mongering or even outright coercion. It is all about perception control. It is big business. When big corporations promote their brands through advertisements, they endeavour to create a positive perception about them and their product. This has led to the unethical claim by most adverts that they are number one in the business, although no formal competition was instituted to determine this. It is not uncommon to find two or more radio stations from the same state claiming to be the number one station. Detergents do this as well, along with newspapers, transporters, you name it. They all claim to be the number-one brand in their respective business.

In a like manner, creating the perception that the Bible is the infallible word of the holy God was the only way to suppress the book's inherent flaws, thereby preventing the inquisitive mind from investigating it. Who in their right mind does not fear to question God? None, I presume. Many people were taught from a very young age that the Bible is the word of the Almighty God. As a result very few are prepared to question anything that is written therein.

It is common knowledge that the Bible did not fall from heaven already bound by God as a manual to life on earth. If it were supposed to be the manual, then one could argue that God should have given it to the so-called first people, Adam and Eve. Instead, it only appeared after several millennia. Adam never saw a copy of it.

Significantly, the Bible was a product of debate by religious scholars and the church fathers several thousands of years later. To this day, there is no universal agreement on what should constitute the 'holy Bible' or 'holy canon'. To complicate things further, the conflicts amongst the

Abrahamic religions are palpable. The Jews, Protestant Christians, and Catholic Christians each have their own version of the Bible. Not to mention, the Muslims have their Quran and different versions of Islam.

The Catholic Bible has 73 books: 46 in the Old Testament and 27 in the New Testament. The Protestant Bible has 66 books, with only 39 in the Old Testament. The books missing from the Protestant Bible are Tobit, Judith, Baruch, Wisdom, Sirach, 1 and 2 Maccabees, and parts of Esther and Daniel. They are called the 'Deuterocanonical' books by Catholics and 'Apocrypha' by Protestants. Martin Luther is alleged to have unilaterally removed the 'Deuterocanonical' books from the Old Testament and placed them in an appendix during the Reformation. They remained in the appendix of the Protestant Bible until about 1826, and then they were removed altogether. There are a lot more other new testament gospels left out of both versions, as well.

For the first three hundred years of Christianity, there was no Bible as we know it today. Christians had the Old Testament Septuagint and literally hundreds of other books from which to choose. The Septuagint, or LXX, was translated from Hebrew to Greek and completed by Jewish scholars in about 148 BC, and it had all of the books, including the ones removed by Martin Luther over 1650 years later. The Catholic Church realized early on that she had to decide which of these books were inspired and which weren't. There were heated debates among theologians, bishops, and church fathers for several centuries. During this time, several church councils, or synods, convened to deal with the matter.

Meetings of note are Rome in 382 AD, Hippo in AD 393, and Carthage in both AD 397 and AD 419. The debates sometimes became bitter on both sides. One of the most famous was between St. Jerome, who felt the seven books were not canonical, and St. Augustine, who said they were.

The one pertinent question that remains is how the spirit of God could debate whether God's writings were inspired or not. How could the spirit of God lead Martin Luther to remove some books from the Old Testament 1650 years later. Which one is the authentic bible? Is it the Jewish Bible, the Catholic Bible, or the Protestant Bible? The disputes about this are endless, even to this day. That is why humanity is being coerced to disregard knowledge and use belief instead. If you do not believe that the Bible is the word of God, then you are deemed worthy of eternal damnation. There is certainly something wrong.

One thing is crystal clear: there is no definite 'thus saith the LORD' in this whole circus. Therefore, the claim that the Bible (whichever one) is the holy word of God is clearly unsustainable. It is a delusion. We know that the stakes are too high to rescind this claim because it has become big business world-wide, but that should not matter. Truth must prevail. Let lies stop, and let the truth set us free. We need to be released from the bondage of this manipulative claim. This misinformation cannot, and should not, be passed on to our children anymore. Enough is enough.

Probably the worst claim of them all is that the Bible is infallible; that is to say, it is not capable of being wrong. While we find it easy to acknowledge that no human being is perfect, somehow we seem to find perfection in a human product – the Bible.

We are told to 'just believe'. Not to question but to just believe. If you happen to have questions about the authenticity of the Bible, you are made to feel guilty about it. You are 'reminded' that you are too sinful to understand the things of God. You must repent and be baptised. Just pretend. Just believe. Just conjure up the experience of 'salvation'. Just believe. Think with your heart. Do not use your brain. You are told that common sense is ungodly because the carnal mind is enmity against God. You must disengage your thinking faculties and go with the flow. That is then credited to you as righteousness.

The initial sin was eating the forbidden fruit, we are told. The new sin is lack of belief in Jesus of Nazareth. It carries the death penalty. In the beginning, we are told, mankind was condemned because they ate of the forbidden tree. Now mankind will be doomed only if they fail to believe in Jesus of Nazareth. Humans are going to die, not because of their sins, but because of their unbelief. They cannot die of their sins anymore because all sins were supposedly paid for by the blood of Jesus of Nazareth. But if a debt is fully paid for, one cannot pay again.

What is the necessity of introducing the precondition of belief then? Why did God not just announce, 'My children, all your sins have been paid for by the death of Jesus of Nazareth. My wrath has been quenched. I am appeased. Therefore, you are all going to be changed so you sin no more.' He could have set a perfect example. As it stands, the God of the Bible cannot be a good example of a forgiver. How does one punish the offender first and then forgive later? How can one receive full payment for the debt first and then claim to have written off the debt later? Punishment is meant to atone for sin. Forgiveness is meant to save you from punishment. Either you punish or you forgive, but surely you cannot do both.

If we were to follow God's example, that would even mean punishing our children continually for sins they committed during their formative years. If, for instance, a child sneaked into the kitchen and helped themselves to a teaspoonful of sugar during their kindergarten years, we would give them a life-long curse for it and also claim later to have forgiven them. If humanity's suffering and death today are punishment for sin, then God has never forgiven. Remember the difference between punishment and a natural consequence.

If not believing in Jesus of Nazareth is a sin, then why can't his blood atone for it? Is he not the one famed for saying, 'Forgive them, Father, for they know not what they are doing'? In other words, he acknowledged that they believed they were doing the right thing even while they were doing the wrong thing. So why can't those who do not believe in Jesus of Nazareth be forgiven? Is it not that they know not what they do? If his death paid off the sin debt to God, why must others be excluded on the flimsy basis of such a speculative concept as belief? Remember, belief is a form of ignorance. It is not knowledge. Why, then, must lack of belief in Jesus of Nazareth be the ultimate sin? Belief and hope sustain you while you wait for truth to manifest. When truth arrives, you gain knowledge, and there is no more need to believe. The fact that we are being asked to 'only believe'

'spiritual Jews' for God to accept them into his kingdom. Surely the claim that the Jews are God's chosen nation on earth has no merit at all. It cannot be validated by Mother Nature and the eternal attributes of God. It is clearly a human invention.

The claim that Jesus of Nazareth is the only way to God is equally baseless. It needs to be investigated. If Jesus of Nazareth is the cosmic master, then he could not have issued such an untrue statement. This must surely be the work of an overzealous writer. God is inexhaustible, and one can never exhaust the ways of, and ways to, God.

One of the tragedies of the Bible is that so many human assertions are attributed to God even though they clearly contradict his character. Probably the greatest tragedy of them all is that humans must just swallow whole everything written in the Bible, under the guise of belief in God, even if their common sense detects the contradiction. That is why humans are encouraged to shut off their common sense and move forward by blind faith.

One more critical observation: The Bible seems to imply that the age of the universe is around six thousand years. Yet there is empirical evidence that there was human life on earth a couple million years ago, not to mention the age of rocks. The Turkana boy or Nariokotome boy of Kenya is a prime example. According to Wikipedia, the Turkana skeleton is 'a nearly complete skeleton of a hominin youth who lived during the early Pleistocene. This specimen is the most complete early human skeleton ever found. It is believed to be between 1.5 and 1.6 million years old. The skeleton was discovered in 1984 by Kamoya Kimeu, a member of a team led by Richard Leakey, at

Nariokotome near Lake Turkana in Kenya'. The oldest human remains found in Kenya are estimated to be seven million years old, making Kenya the new cradle of humankind. As such, it replaces Ethiopia, whose oldest human remains are estimated to be about 4.5 million years old.

It would therefore appear that the Bible is just concerned about the six-thousand-year period covering what I can call the Jewish Dynasty. From creation to Jesus is four thousand years, and from Jesus to the present day is about two thousand years. By making Adam, who was created only six thousand years ago, the father of humankind, the Bible implies that the area around the Euphrates and Tigris rivers (present day Iraq) is the cradle of humankind. We now know that this is not true. The Bible is clearly a Jewish book and not a universal book.

The problem is not the book. The problem is the claims made about the book and the intention behind those claims. There are two very dangerous words used to sustain the claims: 'only' and 'better'. There are two basic ideas that feed these illusions. The first one is the idea expressed by the word 'only' – in the context of having a monopoly. The second idea, which is equally poisonous, is expressed by the word 'better'. – not in the context of improvement, but in the context of inherent superiority.

In the Merriam-Webster dictionary, the word 'only' is defined as 'peerless: alone in a class or category: existing with no other or others of the same kind'. 'Better' is defined as 'superior' in the context of being inherently superior.

This has led to divisive, illusionary claims such as 'Ours is the only true religion. Our God is the only true God. Our way is the only way to God. Our nation is better than the rest' and so on. The world would be healed if we embraced the idea represented by the word 'different' instead and realised that it is this diversity that defines divinity. No part of divinity should ever be considered for elimination.

Different but equal. Equivalent in value but not in quantity, form, shape, or composition.

Just as I am a husband to my wife and a father to my children, so is the president to his wife and children. We are absolutely equal in this regard. We are not the same but equal. We simply are different, but none is better than the other. That is why death treats us equally. Death is God, and God has no favour. Favouritism is a function of imperfection – in particular, selfishness. It cannot be an attribute of God.

The idea represented by the word 'only' has caused enormous damage to the cause of humanity. The sooner we embrace the idea represented by the word 'different', the healthier we shall become. In like manner, the sooner we discard the pursuit of 'better', the sooner we will genuinely collaborate as equals while embracing our diversity and compensating for each other's deficiencies.

Therefore, let these eternal truths guide us:

- All nations are equal before God.
- All religions are equal before God.
- All cultures are equal before God.
- All colours are equal before God.

- All peoples are equal before God.
- There is no need to convert anyone to another's religion.
- There is no need to demonise other peoples' ancestors.
- No nation or religion holds a monopoly on knowledge of God.
- We are all equal although we are different.
- Equality does not mean uniformity or same-ness.
- We should all strive to reach our full potential for the benefit of the whole and not in pursuit of being better than others.
- We are never in competition but in collaboration.
- What humans call good and evil are the two balancing pillars of divinity, which are never at war.

We could go on and on.

If we could truly understand the harmony between evil and good, that would go a long way in saving us from the illusion of a heaven, where only good dwells, and a hell, where only evil dwells. We would then realise that paradise is what we already have, and it is where good and evil live together, side by side, permanently. Whatever we choose to do at any given time is a function of which part of ourselves we wish to express – whether good or evil, because we are both. That is who we are – good and evil. That is what life is – positive and negative, continuously swinging like a pendulum in search of equilibrium. To eliminate evil is to stop life, just as to stop the sun from

This 'perfect place' will be free from work. There's only feasting and worshiping. There will be no need to dig down to find precious metals because gold will be street material, we are told.

Crucially, it is a place where you must surrender forever the freedom of choice. There is no more sense of good and evil. The only thing you are exposed to is the 'good'. No more choice. You must become a robot, a stooge. Just eat, sit, praise, and worship. But if praise and worship become a function of instinct, then they lose their lustre. For praise and worship to be of any value, they must be a function of deliberate choice. For humans to be controlled by instinct means that humanity will go back to God and say we do not want responsibility anymore. Take it back. We want to be like the rest of the animal kingdom – live with no accountability. You, God, must do it all. No more obedience, because obedience is a function of choice. All we want is instinctive compliance. Those who want to go to this heaven must be prepared to surrender their freedom of choice and, with it, the essence of humanity.

Remember, God is said to have made it abundantly clear from the beginning that he cannot tolerate a humanity that knows good and evil, and also lives forever. Mankind can only have one of the two. Therefore, for mankind to live forever, he must be changed to a 'slave of righteousness' first. He must first relinquish the knowledge of good and evil and thereby lose the freedom to choose. God has no problem with such a being living forever. However, without freedom of choice, we lose the essence of being creative beings. There is no creativity in heaven. God has done everything already. That is what

Paul meant when he said, 'we will all be changed—in a flash, in the twinkling of an eye'. That is heaven for you.

However, there is no agreement as to when this change from mortality to immortality will happen. While Paul said this change happens at the resurrection, John saw the river of life flowing from the throne of God, straddled by the tree of life which bears twelve different kinds of fruits per year and whose leaves would be used to heal the nations. John's version seems to be consistent with the original narrative that eternal life comes from eating the fruit of life, but Paul's assertion that it will happen in a flash at the sound of the last trumpet seems consistent with the all too common dogmatic declarations. Either way, the bottom line remains that there is no enterprise in heaven. It is only good as a holiday resort.

The idea of walking on streets of gold is especially revealing. Why would walking on gold be an incentive? I think people forget that gold is one of the least needed materials for human survival. If we would care to be observant, Mother Nature teaches us that the most important things in life were created in abundance – things like the air we breathe, the water we drink, the vegetation, and the soil. For instance, let us compare gold with soil. If one has an acre of soil and another has an acre of pure gold, the one with soil can plant fruit trees and vegetables to survive. The one with an acre of gold cannot grow anything, even if it rains well. That person will eventually starve to death. Gold is only helpful if you can sell it so that you buy life's necessities. Where do you sell it in heaven? After all, it is said flesh and blood will not enter heaven. Who would enjoy walking in the streets when they can just fly around? The bottom line is that, in the absence of the present illusion of scarcity, gold has no value. Therefore, surely gold cannot be an incentive to go to heaven. Even here on earth, we have seen how prices of this so-called precious metal drops when there is over-supply on the world market.

The other promise of heaven is eternal life. The illusion here is that we will live forever in the flesh. This is furthered by the misunderstanding of the state of the dead. Humanity already has eternal life because the spiritual person never dies. Only the physical body dies because it has a lifespan.

The spiritual person is an inter-planetary being that lives forever as part of the cosmos. When a human being dies, only the physical body becomes a corpse. The spirit returns to God alive. God does not keep dead spirits, waiting to resurrect them for the judgement. Spirits are immortal because they do not decompose. They are celestial bodies, not physical ones. You can have souls or spirits of dead people, but you cannot have dead souls or dead spirits.

Flesh and blood is not allowed in heaven because it cannot travel the astronomical distances of the cosmos. The physical body is just a temporary 'house' for the spiritual person to interact with the physical word. The key concept is frequency. The two worlds operate at different frequencies. The physical world is three-dimensional (3-D) whereas the spiritual is four-dimensional (4-D). All 3-D organisms with life in them have a life cycle – they begin, grow, mature, end, and then decompose. There are no physical bodies in heaven because there is no growth. That is why Jesus even went a step further and said there is no sex or marriage in heaven when he addressed the question on spousal inheritance. Paul, for all his confusion, realizes the contradiction when he says, 'We do not know what we shall become, but we shall be changed ... mortality puts on immortality'. The human obsession is to want to keep the physical body, but it is not necessary.

The other bizarre promise of heaven is the absence of sin. What is sin, if one may ask? In simple terms, sin is breaking the law. Unless there is no law in heaven, then there is no sin. It is important to realise that sin exists before it is committed. It is perceived beforehand, and this perception necessitates enactment of the law to define the parameters for sin. Sin, like energy, exists in two states, namely potential (at rest) and kinetic (in motion). Just like a volcano, it exists before it erupts. Once law and order are envisaged and the law is enacted, sin already exists like a dormant volcano, like potential energy in a stretched elastic object. How then can you have order without the law? Unless, of course, there is no order in heaven. Sin is not physical but spiritual. It is abstract and is relative to prior enactment of the law. What is not a sin today may be a sin tomorrow if that particular activity becomes outlawed.

Remember, the first 'sin' was rebellion against the order in the chain of command. Sin and the law are inseparable sides of the same coin. The moment you enact a law, automatically you create the potential to break it — that is sin. Once you say, 'do not do this', the potential to do it is already there; thus, sin is already waiting in the wings. You cannot burn sin with fire. You can only eliminate sin by removing the law. Sin is created by the law, it is defined by the law, and it resides in the law. If heaven is truly a sinless place, then it must be a lawless and order-less place.

The other interesting feature of this heaven is that it has an Israelite city, Jerusalem – albeit a new one. It has twelve gates, representing the twelve tribes of Israel, and each of their names is written on its dedicated gate. It has twelve foundations representing the twelve Apostles. God Almighty is said to dwell and rule in the city. There is no sun, no sea, no sorrow, no pain, no night, and a long list of wishes. It is like an exclusive Israeli club. It is a place for Christians, with no room for other religions. By inference, God Almighty must be a Christian. Nothing is further from the truth.

The truth is that God is all-encompassing. He is the all-in-all. Every religion is in him, by him, and for him. Christianity is just a tiny part of the cosmos's religions just like the earth itself is a tiny and almost invisible part of the universe.

The biblical heaven is an Israeli dream to rule the world. In the final analysis, it is about political power on earth. It follows the old illusion that the earth is the centre of the universe, both in physical location and purpose. We all know now that this is not true.

The God of diversity would never live in such a confined construction, either in the physical realm or in the abstract. The purpose of diversity is not competition. It is to give us experiential context. All experience is relative. You must be surrounded by something different from yourself in order to experience who you are. For you to feel cold, your body must be warmer than the area around you; likewise, for you to feel hot, your body must be colder than your environs. Beauty is a function of contrast. If everything were the same, there would be no beauty, no knowledge, no experience, and, ultimately, no meaning. The quest for superiority is fatalistic, but embracing diversity enhances life.

One of the most bizarre claims is that the world is what it is today because of sin. It is said to have spiralled out of God's control so much that he regrets making humans. How much more can one insult the Supreme Being than that? Now God must invent a plan of salvation for those he himself barred from eating from the tree of life. He must pretend to die on the cross because he cannot simply forgive and move on without shedding blood.

Humanity must believe, against all odds, that one Jesus of Nazareth of the tribe of Judah was in fact the son of God although his mother was married to Joseph. Some even have the cheek to claim that he was fully human and fully divine. Some kind of a hybrid being, I suppose. If he was fully divine, then surely he was only pretending to be human. That would make him fully human and not divine at all because it is humans who pretend.

These untruths are cunningly covered up as God's mystery beyond human comprehension. If they are really beyond human comprehension, why then preach them to humans? Or, worse still, judge them for not understanding. We seem to see history repeating itself. The same God who gave a command to humans who could not decode it in the garden, now asks humans to accept something beyond their comprehension – Jesus of Nazareth. If they don't, they will be condemned to death. It is like giving chickens a lecture on Pythagoras' theorem and decreeing that those chickens who fail a test on the topic will be slaughtered mercilessly.

To add to the confusion, Jesus must retain the genealogy of Joseph in order to be part of the chosen nation of Israel. God the creator has a chosen nation? And this chosen nation is authorised by God to butcher the not-chosen nations and dispossess them of their lands? They must take over the land of the Canaanites, effectively making God the author of colonisation.

If you dare question any of these claims, you are branded a rebel, and you deserve to be thrown in hell and burn there for eternity. You must recant any truthful knowledge or risk condemnation. You must keep the truth to yourself and do like Galileo who, according to popular legend, allegedly muttered the rebellious phrase 'and yet it moves' (Eppur si muove) after his abjuration. Then you are declared righteous and get the reward of eternal life in a paradise called heaven, where there is no sin, death, or suffering. And this is supposed to be the way of God. Or more aptly, wicked ways of a holy God.

CHAPTER 11

JESUS OF NAZARETH – THE MAN ON A NON-EXISTENT MISSION

Jesus of Nazareth's existence is a historical fact. He is not a myth. Neither is he folklore. There is empirical evidence all over to authenticate this. However, the claims about his identity, deeds, and mission need exploration. His main mission is said to be the reconciliation of mankind with God. He is said to have come to die in order to atone for mankind's sins – all sins. God would be appeased and then reconcile with mankind. The complete plan, we are told, was hatched in heaven in great detail but executed on earth secretly.

Why was Jesus' mission such a huge secret? The Old Testament people believed he was coming to set up an earthly kingdom. Surely there should have been attempts to clarify beyond all doubt the real mission of the Messiah. He himself is quoted as instructing his disciples not to tell anyone that he was the Messiah. When Pilate asked him if he was the king of the Jews, Jesus cunningly confirmed it, and they killed him for that claim. He committed treason. What is critically important is that he confirmed that he was the king of the Jews. Not of the whole world. He was rightfully labelled as 'king of the Jews' by a placard hung above his head on the cross. It is this secret mission that people are asked to believe or else burn in hell. Just as humanity thought that their troubles with the law were over, a more difficult precondition for acceptance with God was introduced: belief in a God-man from Nazareth. It is no longer about knowledge; it is about ignorance. So mankind is now rewarded for being reckless enough to 'just believe'.

Mankind was not made explicitly aware of what was happening. When Peter said Jesus was the Messiah, Jesus told him that flesh and blood did not reveal this to him except his father in heaven. He exhorted his disciples not to tell anyone that he was the Messiah. Even though the Jews expected a Messiah to come, his mission was not made clear to them either. They thought he was supposed to set up a Jewish kingdom on earth. Were they wrong? No. They were right. Jesus himself admitted to Pilate that he was the king of the Jews. (Not king of the world.) Even when the 'angel' appeared to Joseph in that famous dream, he instructed him to name the child Jesus because he would save 'his' people, not 'all' people, from their sins. Who are his people? The Jews. He is of the lineage of David, of the tribe of Judah.

The notion that humanity needs a saviour is the source of all of this misinformation. For a start, humanity was never separated from God at any one moment in its history. It is impossible to be separated from God and continue to live. Even in a hypothetical situation where separation from God were possible, humans would no longer exist, even as corpses. Everything (physical and spiritual) in the universe is sustained by God. Even a decomposing corpse is sustained by God because decomposition is energy changing from one form to another. It is another form of life. A 'dead' body has life in it. That is why 'dead' meat gives energy to a living body to sustain *its* life. God cannot be separated from humanity.

Even in the erroneous narrative of the Bible, to prove that God was never separated from mankind by 'sin', he actually made clothes from animal skins instead of saying, 'We are now separate'. He did not say blood would be needed to reconcile. Also, later we hear that he spoke face to face with Moses, Abraham, and a host of other patriarchs and prophets. Remember, even in the Genesis narrative of the fall, mankind never actually sinned against God. He had no capacity to sin. The separation is imaginary.

So, how could Jesus of Nazareth come to reconcile that which was never separated in the first place? Even the biblical narrative cannot sustain this error. Let us look at a few examples:

1. We are told that God made and gave mankind clothes from animal skins when mankind sinned. Where is the separation here if God can still bring them clothes? Maybe the supposed banning of man from the Garden of Eden is what is referred to as separation from God, but the Garden of Eden is not God. It is a place. God does not stay

in the Garden of Eden. Access to the tree of life should not have anything to do with sin because it was never part of the original deal. It was God's unilateral decision to prevent man from accessing it – as an afterthought.

2. It is recorded that God spoke with Moses face to face. He is said to have given him tablets of stone with commandments engraved by his own hand. Where is the separation?

3. It is also recorded that Abraham got instructions directly from God to leave his ancestral land and later to sacrifice his son. Where is the separation?

4. Enoch is said to have walked with God to the point of being raptured. Where is the separation?

5. Numerous prophets received instructions directly from God: Elijah, Elisha, Ezekiel, Samuel the priest, and more. Where is the separation from God?

6. Jesus of Nazareth is also called Immanuel, meaning 'God with us'. If he went even a step further and stayed in the womb of a woman, as claimed, then where is the separation?

God has never been separated from any of his creation, let alone, from humanity. This whole claim should be repudiated as a matter of urgency.

Therefore, the so-called plan of salvation is clearly non-existent.

CHAPTER 12

CONCLUSION

The Christian Bible cannot be, and should not be, regarded as the infallible word of God, the Supreme Being, because of the following:

1. The story of creation is riddled with factual errors consistent with the author's misconceptions about the universe at the time of writing. The most prominent one is the illusion that the earth is the biggest body in the universe and is flat and stationary. This has since become obsolete. God could not have inspired incorrect information.

2. Evidence regarding the authorship of the book of Genesis and other influential books is inconclusive.

3. The Bible did not fall from heaven; rather, it was written by many authors and was compiled by humans through debate.

4. It contains folklore presented as historical events.

5. God is not the author of confusion. Therefore, the story of the Tower of Babel as the source of human languages is clearly untrue. It is a legend.

6. The illusion that God has been separated from humanity is unsustainable because that separation can never happen while mankind continues to exist. Therefore the so-called plan of salvation is purely a human creation.

I further notice that the God of the Bible cannot be the Supreme Being, the creator of the universe if he really is what the Bible portrays him to be:

1. A liar, because he claimed to have made man in his own image while, in actual fact, he created people who did not know good and evil and could not live forever.

2. A pretender, because he is just pretending to fight with the devil, who is less powerful. He pretended to be a baby in a human womb, pretended to be a man, pretended to be weak enough to be captured by humans, pretended to die so that he could then pretend to have risen from the dead, pretended to have defeated physical death, and ultimately pretended to have purchased reconciliation with mankind.

3. Unforgiving, because he was so unwilling to forgive that his 'only son' had to die to atone for sin.

4. Insecure, because he had to create languages in order to confuse people to safeguard himself.

5. Vengeful, because he had to pronounce all sorts of curses on his creation when he was wronged. He even prepared a place of torture called hell, where sinners will be tormented for eternity. He is a serial punisher.

6. Unjust, because he has a chosen nation – Israel – which is allowed to dispossess other nations of their land.

7. Fearful of being judged by humans, causing him not to deal decisively with Satan in the beginning, in the hopes of proving that he was a just God so angels and humans would worship him out of love not fear. All this was at a huge cost to humans.

8. A flip-flopper. At one point, he was happy that he made man. At another point, he regretted it deeply. At one point, he made an everlasting covenant with Abraham. At another point, he made a new covenant with Israel. At one point, he punished mankind and the rest of creation for sin. At another point, he claimed to want atonement for the same sin so that he could claim to have forgiven it. At one point, he said mankind must die because of sin. At another point, the same mankind must be resurrected in order to be tortured in hell for eternity. At one point, he gave mankind dominion on earth. At another point, he wants to set up an everlasting kingdom on earth with himself as king. At one point, he gave Cain and Abel diversity of talent and vocation. At another time, he rejected Cain's offering for no reason, in preference of Abel's. He is the same

God who hates Esau for no reason and loves Jacob regardless of his flawed character. He is the same God who made diverse nations and languages but then made Israel a chosen nation and requires all other nations to strive to become 'spiritual Israelites'. On the one hand, he claims to have forgiven mankind's sins while, on the other hand, he has received full payment for the same sins at the cross of Calvary. At one point, he creates a rainbow as a sign that he would never destroy the world again. At another point, he promises to destroy the whole world with fire. At one point, he created a perfect world where all creatures lived in harmony and ate only vegetation. Then at a later point, he was forced to convert some creatures into predators and others into prey. He had to redesign the physical features of these creatures, as well as their digestive systems.

9. A mortal being, because he died on the cross.
10. A false accuser, because he claimed that humans sinned against him when they did not have the capacity to sin.
11. An impostor, because he claimed to have hatched a plan of salvation for a non-existent separation.

We do not live in order to go to heaven. We live in order to express who we are: human beings. That is our identity, and, by our fruits, you shall know us. An apple tree bears apples to feed other organisms, not to go to heaven. It continues to bear fruit year in and year out, regardless of whether humans are thankful or not. The motivation is not its future fate but its present identity.

This idea that we live in order to go to heaven is actually alien to humanity. It was only introduced a few thousand years ago by a small section of humans. To our side of the world, Africa, it was brought by Christianity and Islam. Africans had never lived in order to go to heaven previously. Doing good was our highest virtue – an expression of our identity – and still is. We do not need to go to heaven because heaven is where we are if we choose to experience it. The same goes for hell. We know very well the difference between life in the physical realm and life in the spiritual realm. We understand that anything in the physical realm that reproduces itself has a life span. It is born, matures, reproduces, and then dies to leave space for its offspring. We are therefore aware that physical death is actually desirable. Only premature death is undesirable. We are also fully aware that heaven and hell, as physical destinations, are an illusion, and the desire for immortality of the physical body is like chasing after the wind.

The gospel of heaven and hell is ultimately just fear-mongering, and the effect is that humans fear hell more than they love heaven. The gospel of heaven without the fear of hell would find very few takers. Humans primarily prefer to live on earth. Even God knows that very well. Heaven is of secondary interest to them, and it only becomes attractive when compared to the horror of hell.

Good life is all that humans want, and they would rather have that good life on earth. They don't really desire to live forever in the flesh; rather, their desire is to live a comfortable, happy life to a ripe old age. They want the freedom to enjoy life, to have sex, to play games, to invent machines, to overcome challenges, to be adventurers, and to use their God-given brains. Humans are not angels; they do not like the idea of praise and worship all day long. They were not made for that. They love enterprise and productive work. Taking humans to heaven is not salvation at all because humans love their earth and were designed to live on earth. Besides, changing humans to be like angels would be an admission of failure by God. That would confirm that he was wrong to make humans in the first place. If God were to take humans to heaven, he would do so from a point of weakness, not strength.

We are told that the so-called plan of salvation is beyond human comprehension. Therefore, we are expected to just swallow everything – hook, line, and sinker. The paradox is that if it is really beyond human comprehension, why preach it to humans at all? Worse still is to judge them for not understanding it. This fear-mongering must just stop. We have had enough of it.

In the final analysis, it is my humble suggestion that the Christian Bible, with all its glaring factual inaccuracies on key issues such as creation and the character of God, should not be regarded as the infallible word of God. By extension, the God of the Bible seems to be a very small version of the Supreme Being. He is an Israelite God and not the God of the universe. He seems very weak and biased.

Therefore, the Christian Bible and the Christian God should never be forced down the throats of non-Israelites. Christianity still owes the world an apology for millennia of misinformation and oppression. Pope John Paul II asked for forgiveness from God on behalf of Christianity for this but did not apologise directly to the affected ethnic groups themselves. This is contrary to Jesus's teaching in Mathew 5: 23–4 (NIV):

> [23]'Therefore, if you are offering your gift at the altar and there remember that your brother or sister has something against you, [24]leave your gift there in front of the altar. First go and be reconciled to them; then come and offer your gift.'

Christianity must apologise to affected ethnic groups first before they go to the altar to ask for God's forgiveness. The time to do so is now. The most important thing after the apology is to ensure that the misinformation is discontinued. Never again must non-Israelites be taught Israeli doctrines as the bona fide word of God.

I am convinced beyond any reasonable doubt that the story of the biblical forbidden tree is folklore.

Let every nation walk in the presence of their God without fear of condemnation.

To God Almighty, the Supreme Being, be the glory.

ABOUT THE AUTHOR

Jabulani Midzi is a natural leader, teacher, manager, and motivational speaker. He is passionate about service and subscribes to the ideal that we are all part of one great whole. As such, whatever talent one has should be utilized to the benefit of humanity. To him, the purpose of life is not competition but collaboration.

Printed in the United States
By Bookmasters